When RACING *Was* RACING

First published in 2012

A catalogue record for this book is available from the British Library

ISBN: 978-0-857331-83-0

Published by Haynes Publishing, Sparkford, Yeovil,
Somerset BA22 7JJ, UK
Tel: 01963 442030 Fax: 01963 440001
Int. tel: +44 1963 442030 Int. fax: +44 1963 440001
E-mail: sales@haynes.co.uk
Website: www.haynes.co.uk

Haynes North America Inc., 861 Lawrence Drive,
Newbury Park, California 91320, USA

Creative Director: Kevin Gardner
Designed for Haynes by BrainWave

Printed and bound in the US

When RACING *Was* RACING

A Century of Horse Racing

Adam Powley

Contents

Introduction

Horse racing is ingrained in sporting history, and no more so than in Britain. So intrinsic is the sport in our nation's past and present, that it has become part of the landscape, our culture and our language. To "win hands down", "dark horse" and "ringer" are all terms that originated in racing, and have become part of everyday conversation. Racecourses can be found up and down the country, ranging from oases of green turf in the midst of urban areas to magnificent parks set in some of the most beautiful countryside in the land.

In common with so many sports, racing is now big business. It is estimated to be worth £3.7 billion to the UK economy and around £10 billion is spent on betting on the sport each year. Nearly 100,000 people are either directly or indirectly employed in the industry. Its key dates – the Derby, the Grand National, the Cheltenham Gold Cup to name just a few – are among the most established, important and popular in the sporting calendar.

For all its modern success, however, it is the sport's past that really enchants and enthrals many of its devotees. Today's racing unquestionably provides superb entertainment, but it is the thrill and character of the sport in bygone days that, for many people, is not quite matched by its modern-day equivalent. In some people's eyes, racing is just not what it used to be.

This book is all about the marvellous past of British racing. The figures given apply to racing in the UK – the way newspapers operated with a focus on stories at home determines that – and in doing so celebrates the great races, the champion thoroughbreds, the famous jockeys and the memorable moments from over a century of racing. It draws on just some of the millions of photographs contained within the wonderful Mirrorpix archive. For over 100 years photographers from the *Daily* and *Sunday Mirror*, the *Sunday People* and a host of associated national and local titles have been on hand to record racing's finest and most exciting moments for posterity. Their work features in this collection to illustrate the legendary stories and achievements down the decades.

Few sports are as visceral as horse racing, and the photos in this book vividly capture the raw physicality of a sport that can test man and beast to the ultimate. But this is not just a roll call of the famous, great and the grand of the "sport of kings". Here are images that evoke racing behind the scenes, its characters and courses, and the offbeat moments that seem to sum up the unique flavour of racing in the past. It is not a rose-tinted look at a mythological past: with its gallery of rascals and less-savoury episodes, horse racing has always had an edgy element to its appeal, and this book reflects that.

But in presenting a broad picture of the sport as it once was, we get a fascinating glimpse of a lost age when the sport had the atmosphere of a pastime not quite so wedded to absolute commercial imperatives (even if the reality might not have been so clear cut). As a window on a "lost world" of horse racing, the photos presented here bring back some wonderful memories of a golden age.

Passing the mile post in the 1955 Derby. Phil Drake was the eventual winner.

Racing's Early Golden Ages: The Ancient World to The 1920s

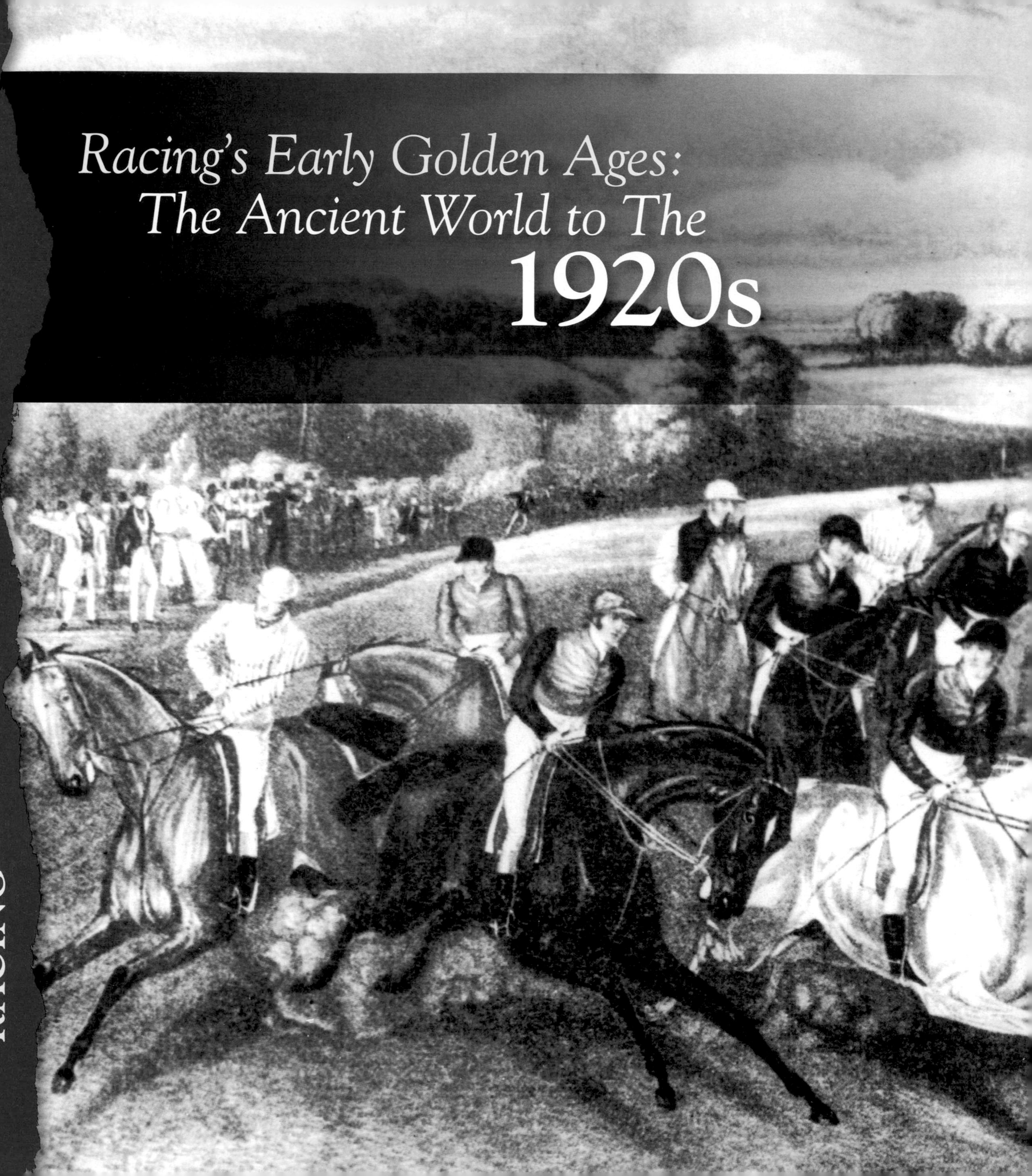

This stylized 1837 illustration of the Derby captures the thrill of the big race.

Horse racing is probably as old as the relationship between humans and tamed wild horses. The domestication of the horse can be traced back to **3000 BCE** but may well have originated earlier. In Central Asia, nomadic tribes utilized the horse for warfare, and specialized skills led to the development of an embryonic form of racing.

In the classical world horse racing had an important position in the sporting calendar – races took place at the ancient Olympics from **638 BCE**. Racing may have been brought to Britain by the Romans after the invasion of **AD 55**; evidence of some form of the sport crops up over the centuries – there are records of races taking place at Smithfield, just outside London, in the **12th century**, and in Chester on public holidays.

The true roots of British horse racing lie in the **17th century** and the reign of James I. James brought his love for racing to England from Scotland when he built a residence near Newmarket, and races sprang up across the country as his successors strengthened the influence of royal patronage. The aristocracy's love of gambling fuelled further development, on-course bookmaking and the need for organization. The formation of the Jockey Club and publication of its calendar in **1752** helped codify the sport, bringing to a close the era of "match racing" when just two horses – invariably owned by competing aristocrats – faced off against each other in races. Instead, multiple competitors ran over shorter distances with a greater focus on speed. The emergence of thoroughbred horses stems from the arrival of three Arabians in England, named after their owners: the Byerley Turk (brought to Britain around **1690**), the Darley Arabian colt (**1704**) and the Godolphin Arabian (foaled in **1724**) – the name that inspired Sheikh Mohammed al Maktoum nearly 260 years later when establishing his stable. Every thoroughbred racehorse since can trace its lineage to these three stallions.

SATURDAY'S RACING.

A one-day meeting at Hurst Park on Saturday wound up a busy week, and concluded the metropolitan fixtures for the flat-racing season. Results :—

Race.	Winner.	Rider.	Price.
T.Y.O. Sell. (16)	Venta..........	Hare	7 to 2
Vyner (15)........	Fleeting Love..	Plant........	100 to 8
Champion N'y (15)	Cherry Pip	Dillon	2 to 1
Hurst P'k A't'm(9)	Scotch Cherry..	Hunter	5 to 2
An All-a'd Sell. (15)	Falcon	Madden	5 to 6
November (6)	Australian Clrs.	Madden......	7 to 1

(The figures in parentheses indicate the number of starters).

Otto Madden, it will be seen, rode two winners. W. Lane had five mounts, but failed to score once, and Madden is thus six points in front of the Falmouth House rider at the top of the winning jockeys' list, the scores now standing: Madden 150, Lane 144.

The following appear to have chances at Warwick to-day, when the events are confined to hurdles and fences: —Wellesbourne Maiden—Ebbsfleet; Hatton Hurdle—Ormeau; Warwick Steeplechase—Dermot Asthore; Upton Steeplechase—De Rougemont; Castle Hurdle—Sprig of Shillelagh; Leamington Steeplechase—Sequel II.

The celebrity of great horses was considerable: the famous equine artist George Stubbs painted the unbeaten and versatile Eclipse as a six-year-old in **1770**. With the advent of the Classic flat races in the latter half of the **18th century**, racing grew in popularity, its appeal given added impetus with the arrival of the railways in the **19th century** and the means for huge crowds to attend big race meetings. The divisions between National Hunt racing over hurdles or fences, and flat races over set distances, led to distinct events. The first official Grand National steeplechase took place in **1839**, while the National Hunt Committee was established in **1866**. By that time handicapping had been introduced, with Admiral Henry John Rous appointed regulator in **1855**. Regulation was a must: in **1844** the identity of the Derby winner Running Rein was later revealed to have been faked in a case of horse-switching: the actual winner had been the four-year-old Maccabeus. The title was eventually awarded to Orlando, who had been runner-up.

In **1879** licences for jockeys were introduced, as the sport became global. Iroquois, the first American-bred horse to win the Derby, was steered home by the great jockey superstar Fred Archer in **1881**. Archer was to tragically commit suicide in **1886**. By **1902**, the filly Sceptre reigned supreme, having won four of the five Classics in just one year.

In **1903** doping was banned after an American race-fixer used cocaine to improve horses' performances. There was shock of a different kind when the filly Signorinetta won the **1908** Derby as a 100–1 shot, following it up with the Oaks two days later. From **1913**, horses older than two had to be known by name. With the advent of the First World War, in contrast to many other sports, racing continued, albeit with some considerable differences: the **1915** and **1917** Nationals were run at Gatwick.

RIGHT: Minoru is led in by owner King Edward VII at Epsom, after winning the 1909 Derby.

LEFT INSET: The earliest mention for horse racing in the fledgling *Daily Mirror*. In the first edition, there was a rather modest rundown of recent results and some very tentative betting advice for the meeting at Warwick.

First run in 1780, the Derby has been a grand social occasion for over two centuries. This print, from around 1850, evokes the carnival atmosphere surrounding the premier Classic.

BELOW: A remarkable early photographic scene from the Derby in 1865. The race was won by the Triple Crown champion Gladiateur III, French-owned and bred but trained in Newmarket. The Grand Prix Imperial was renamed in Gladiateur's honour in 1869, and is still run today.

Putting on the Style

Race going has long provided an opportunity for the well-heeled to show off their wealth and finery, and few racecourses have afforded a more suitable arena than Ascot. Indeed, the course has been central to the social calendar for the English upper classes for centuries, and in the period just before the First World War it was widely reported in the nation's newspapers.

The course itself was founded by royalty. Queen Anne was a keen racing fan, and chose the heathland site near Windsor Castle while out riding in 1711. The very first contest (a series of heats over a distance of 4 miles) was called Her Majesty's Plate, beginning a long association with royalty and the aristocracy; the monarchy still owns the course. The Gold Cup was introduced in 1807; this pivotal race, run over the distance of 2½ miles, has become synonymous with "Ladies Day" and the resultant displays of fashion.

RIGHT: The fashion styles of 1912.

ABOVE: A top hat and cane for the man-about-Ascot in 1912.

BELOW: A glimpse of stocking was a shocking sight in 1913.

THE KING AND QUEEN DRIVE IN SEMI-STATE LONG ASCOT RACECOURSE TO THE ROYAL BOX

ABOVE: Ascot fashion, 1910-style.

LEFT: The *Daily Mirror* reports on the royal procession at Ascot in 1908.

Death at the Derby

One of the most memorable – and infamous – dates in racing history came on 4th June 1913. At the showpiece event of the flat season, a huge crowd gathered on Epsom Downs to witness a Derby of great drama and tragedy. With the suffragette movement's campaign to win the vote for women at its height, a prominent young campaigner called Emily Davison tried to stop the victory of King George V's horse, Anmer.

To gasps and screams from the crowd, Davison was caught under Anmer's hooves and sustained serious injuries. Davison never recovered, and died in hospital four days later.

RIGHT & BELOW: The dramatic moment when Davison and Anmer collided at Tattenham Corner. It is still unclear whether Davison actually intended to end her life, as she was later found to be carrying a return train ticket.

BELOW: The *Daily Mirror* gave relatively scant coverage to Davison's intervention. Indeed, sections of the press devoted more attention to the injuries sustained by the jockey, Herbert Jones.

June 7, 1913 THE DAILY MIRROR. Page 3

LADIES' DAY SEES FEW LADIES AT EPSOM OWING TO THE RAIN.

Rain is apt to spoil pretty hats and dresses, so the attendance of ladies on the course yesterday was not nearly so large as usual. The photographs show some who did attend sheltering under umbrellas, and lunch between the showers.

Davy, the Dublin newsvendor, who always attends the meeting.

Elaborate precautions were taken yesterday to prevent any suffragette outrage. (1) St. Bega's fall in the Oaks. The crowd, as seen, were kept behind the second row of rails. (2) The Derby Day incident, when Miss Davison brought down Anmer, showing the crowd right up to the course.

Although there was no sensational incident such as marked the Derby, the Oaks did not pass off without an accident, Lord Lonsdale's St. Bega falling at Tattenham Corner. R. Crisp, the jockey, was thrown, but fortunately escaped with nothing worse than a shaking.—(*Daily Mirror*, L.N.A. and Sport and General.)

CUSTOMS AUTHORITIES DETAIN RIFLES AND BAYONETS AT BELFAST.

Twelve cases containing about 500 rifles and bayonets have been detained by the Customs authorities at Belfast. (1) Reproduction of one of the labels, which, it will be noticed, were marked "Electrical plant." They were shipped from Manchester. (2) Guarding the cases. The arms were found to be new and of a modern pattern.

LEFT: A view towards the main stand at Epsom c. 1900, as crowds spill onto the course at the conclusion of the race. Note the preponderance of horses and carriages.

BELOW: When he's riding winners … In 1915, 10-year-old jockey George Formby sat astride his father's horse Eliza, with trainer "Mr Schofield" holding on to the reins. George weighed just 3st 13lbs. Minimum weights have since risen, and by the 21st century jockeys have to tip the scales at no less than 7st 12lbs.

Racing's Roaring Decade

THE 1920s

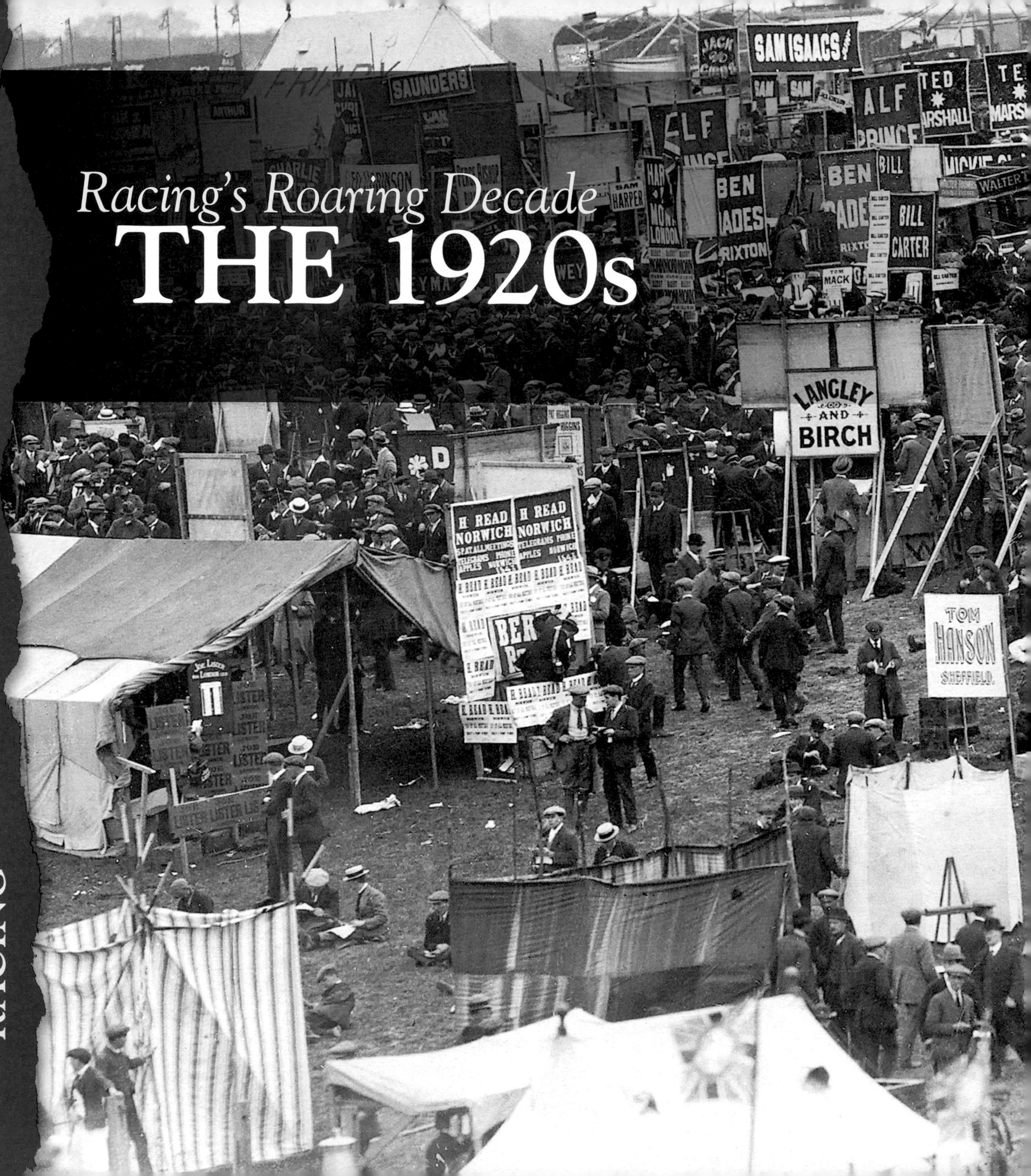

Bookmakers do a roaring trade: the scene at Epsom in 1920.

The 1920s was a tumultuous decade in Britain, following the end of the war. Amid changing times, the public sought the mass spectator entertainments of sport and its premier events in ever-increasing numbers, including racing – and there was plenty of spectacle to keep them thrilled.

In **1920** number cloths were introduced, the same year as the first Prix de l'Arc de Triomphe took place, named in honour of the 1919 Allied victory parade around Paris' famous war memorial. Also in **1920**, Spion Kop won the Derby in record time, followed in **1921** with another heroic performance in the Epsom Classic, this time from Humorist, despite suffering from tuberculosis. Steve Donoghue won the last of his 10 consecutive Champion Jockey titles in **1923**, while Sansovino's win in the **1924** Derby meant that the aristocratic clan after whom the race was named had triumphed for the first time in 137 years.

The Cheltenham Gold Cup made its debut in **1924**, though it took time to evolve into steeplechasing's most prestigious prize and, indeed, at the time the four-mile National Hunt Chase was actually the Cheltenham festival's premier event. In a sure sign of changing times, the Derby was broadcast by the BBC for the first time in **1927**, a year after similar coverage of the Kentucky Derby in America had ushered in a new media age. The sport saw further development in **1926** when a betting tax was introduced by one Winston Churchill. That same year, the famed mare Sceptre, one of the greats of the sport, who had won four of the five Classics in 1902, died.

Scuttle's 1000 Guineas victory in **1928** was a conspicuous though isolated Classics success for owner King George V, but not as headline-grabbing as Tipperary Tim's shock 100–1 win in the National. In an extraordinary renewal Tipperary Tim beat just one other finisher – who had been remounted after falling – in a 42-strong field. Innovation off the track continued. The Racehorse Betting Control Board, later to become the Horserace Totalisator Board, and more popularly known as the "Tote", was established in **1929**. That same year, there were a record 66 starters in the Grand National – and another 100–1 winner in Gregalach.

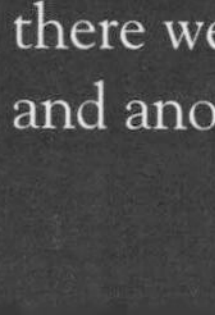

Troytown was a horse prone to mistakes, but with the heart and power of a true champion. He won the 1920 Grand National, despite two severe jumping errors, with jockey Jack Anthony having to virtually cling on for victory. Like Gladiateur, Troytown has a race named in his honour – the Troytown Chase at Navan.

ABOVE: The long and the short of it: in 1920, trainer Stanley Wootton towered over then apprentice jockey Charlie Smirke. The 14-year-old would go on to become one of the great riders.

RIGHT: In an extraordinary three-way dead heat, Dumas, Marvex and Dinkie crossed the winning line at the same time in the Royal Borough Handicap at Windsor in 1923. The outcome was not unique, however: it had occurred in 1857, 1880, 1902 and 1915. Photo-finish facilities have, naturally, prevented this occurring in the modern era.

RACE

Dramatic action shots from the 1920s. At Windsor in 1927 (below), He Will led on his way to victory in the Mill Hurdle. At Plumpton in 1928 (right) the *Mirror*'s photographer brilliantly captured the breathtaking sight of horses clearing a fence during the Portsdale Steeplechase, won by Squire Marten and ridden by Bill Parvin.

LEFT: One of the most poignant of Derby races came in 1921 when Humorist, superbly ridden by Steve Donoghue, won by a neck in a thrilling finish. The victory delighted his connections and his followers, for Humorist was an inconsistent thoroughbred who mixed glittering success with surprising defeats. In the 2000 Guineas a little over a month earlier, he was apparently coasting to victory only to dramatically concede advantage and the race. The reason became clear a few weeks after the Derby. Humorist had been suffering from TB and died from a lung haemorrhage.

LEFT: The first day of Royal Ascot in 1925; Sir Edward Stern made a suitably eye-catching entrance as he arrived in his coach.

LEFT: Eager punters aboard lines of buses craned their necks for a view at Epsom. For hundreds of thousands of Londoners the Derby was the summer's "big day out", and transport companies did profitable business ferrying spectators to the Epsom Downs. The traditional midweek staging was also hugely popular, providing a precious day off work and school.

BELOW: A far cry from the computerized world of modern betting: a modest betting box at Epsom in 1927.

–LEGENDS–

Steve Donoghue

Steve Donoghue was born in the 19th century but emerged as a very modern sporting idol. As a six-time Derby winner, he was immensely popular with the race-going public – "Come on Steve!" became one of the most familiar and loudest cheers well into the mid-1920s. His dashing style, fame and renown arguably surpassed that of Fred Archer, and Donoghue's standing was only really eclipsed by Gordon Richards.

Born in Warrington, Lancashire, Donoghue initially rode in France and Ireland before making his British breakthrough with Henry Persse's Stockbridge stable in 1911. Donoghue steered the famous two-year-old, The Tetrarch, to victories in 1913; The Tetrarch was reputed to be the fastest ever ridden at the time.

Donoghue was synonymous with forging exceptional partnerships and headline-grabbing sequences. He rode the popular stayer Brown Jack, who won the marathon Queen Alexandra Stakes at Royal Ascot an extraordinary six years running. Donoghue lifted a hat-trick of Classics twice in 1915 and 1917, and his three successive Derby wins between 1921 and 1923 confirmed his pre-eminence in the sport. While he could not repeat his success as a jockey when he became a trainer and breeder, his legend remained intact. And he never forgot what underpinned his glittering success. Of the horses he rode Donoghue said, "I think of them as my friends, my greatest friends."

RACING –STATS–

Steve Donoghue

Name: Steve Donoghue

Born: 1884

Died: 1945

Highlights: Six Derby winners; 14 Classics; Champion Jockey 1914–23

RIGHT: Donoghue rides Captain Cuttle to a four-length victory over Tamar in the 1922 Derby. The jockey only accepted the mount on the Friday evening before the race.

ABOVE: As one of the most famous sportsmen of his era, Donoghue was used to rubbing shoulders with other stars. Here he meets Hollywood legend Charlie Chaplin (left) and racing driver Malcolm Campbell.

BELOW: At the 1927 Oaks, Donoghue shared some tips with Lord Lascelles.

Donoghue completed an unprecedented hat-trick of Derby wins in 1923 aboard Papyrus. It was a magnificent achievement, and would have been greater still had he not been beaten the following year by Sansovino. Donoghue restored what appeared to be flat racing's natural order with victory on Manna in 1925, a fourth win in five remarkable years.

LEFT: Small is beautiful: a Mr Whisker of Newmarket earned a reputation in 1922 for making the world's lightest serviceable saddle, weighing just 1lb.

RIGHT: Amid a sea of hats in 1924, Lord Derby led in his horse Sansovino after winning the Blue Riband race named after his ancestor. It was the first victory for the Derby family in 137 years. The race originated after Lord Derby won a coin toss against Lord Bunbury in 1780 to decide in whose honour the race would be named. Lord Bunbury found some compensation with the establishment of the Bunbury Cup, run at Newmarket.

ABOVE & BELOW: Huge crowds flocked to a gloriously sunny Ascot in June 1927.

Spion Kop's lineage proved successful eight years after his own victory when his foal Felstead, previously a modest performer, underwent a meteoric improvement as a three-year-old and won the Derby at 33–1, under the famed hold-up rider Harry Wragg.

Amid a rain-drenched Epsom, the unfancied 33–1 shot Trigo, ridden by apprentice jockey Joe Marshall, won the Derby, beating Walter Gay by 1½ lengths.

War and Peace
THE 1930s-40s

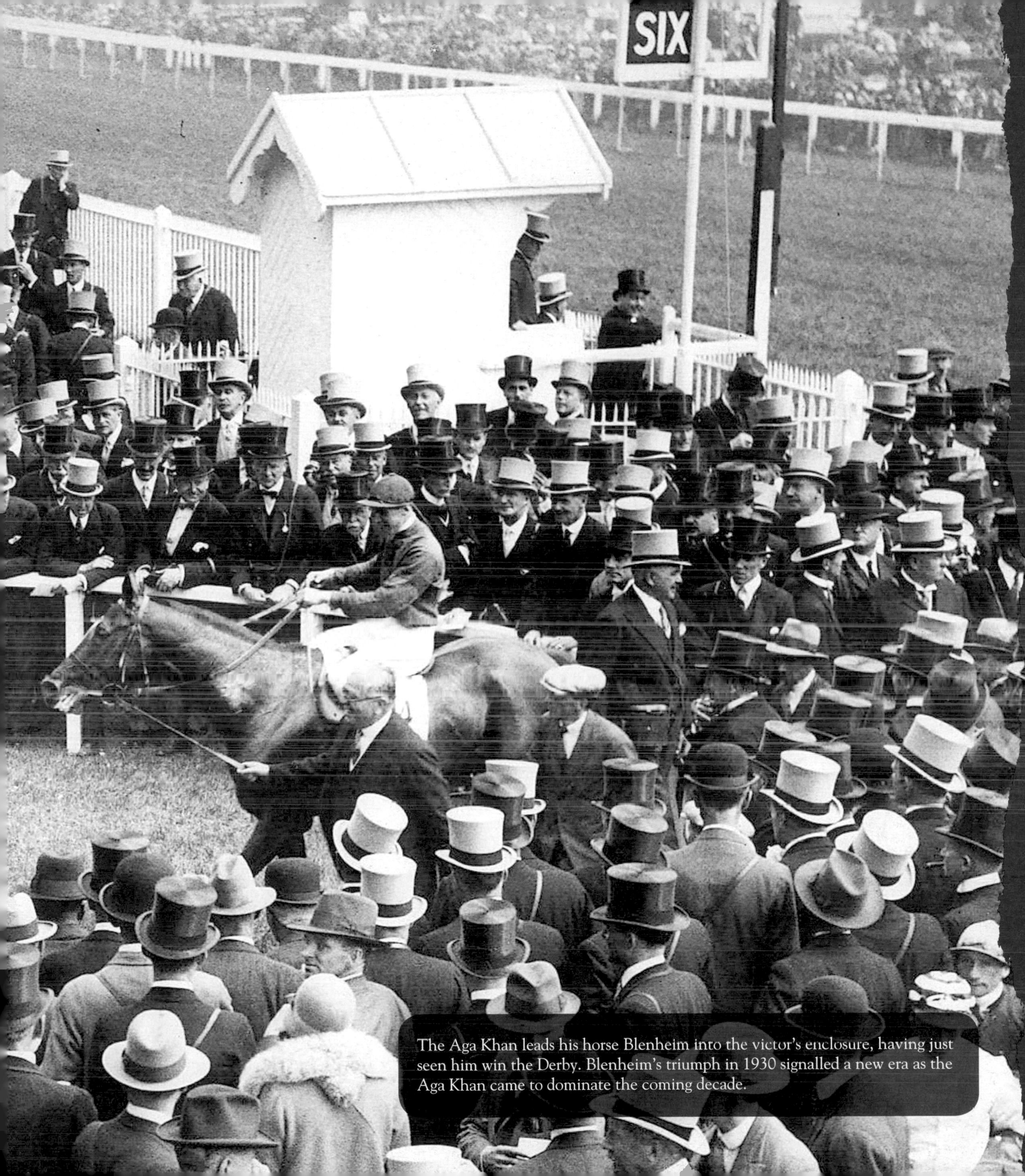

The Aga Khan leads his horse Blenheim into the victor's enclosure, having just seen him win the Derby. Blenheim's triumph in 1930 signalled a new era as the Aga Khan came to dominate the coming decade.

The 1930s saw the emergence of a new generation of leading racing lights, from jockeys to owners, but Gordon Richards just kept on winning, maintaining the impression of business as usual. In the run-up to renewed hostilities at the end of the decade, the sport continued to try to maintain a sense of permanence, but the nature of total war ensured racing did not simply "keep calm and carry on" as normal. The world changed and so did the sport.

Fred Fox's success in winning the **1930** Jockey Championship hinted at the possibility of a new order but Richards was having none of it, and won the crown for the next decade. He would also break Fred Archer's record for most winners in a season in **1933**, ending the season on 259. One legend did call it a day, however, when Steve Donoghue retired in **1937**.

Mahmoud broke the Derby record in **1936**, as the Aga Khan continued to dominate the flat, and in the same year Golden Miller won the Cheltenham Gold Cup for the fifth time in a row. Mid-day Sun's **1937** Derby victory was notable not just for the odds of 100–1 but for the fact that his owner was female.

With war declared, the **1939** Doncaster meeting on 4th September was abandoned, but racing did continue through the conflict, albeit in much reduced circumstances: the St Leger, for example, was run at four different locations.

The Aga Khan sold Bahram and Mahmoud to American stud owners in **1940**, damaging his popularity in Britain. The Grand National was cancelled between **1941** and **1945** to reflect the general gloom, but with the end of war racing boomed, with huge crowds flocking back to courses across the country. They were to see new innovations: in **1947** the photo finish and evening meetings were introduced (the first was held at Hamilton Park), while in **1949** a government commission found that the average spend on betting per household per day was two shillings.

King George V and Queen Mary repeat a seemingly timeless scene, pulled in their carriage by fine white horses at Ascot in 1931.

The Aga Khan beams as he leads in Blenheim, following his 1930 Derby win. The jockey was the great Harry Wragg, who engineered a stunning win with a brilliant tactical race. Wragg became known as the "Head Waiter" on account of such tactics, as he often waited until the last chance to push home his lead.

Windsor Lad beat the much-fancied Colombo to win the 1934 Derby and the same year lifted the St Leger in record time.

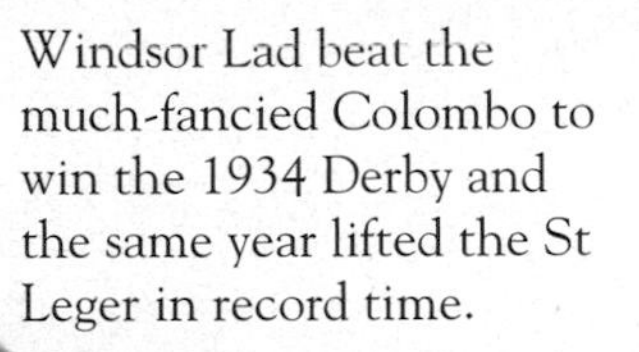

ABOVE: Jockey Joe Childs, who won 15 Classics over a magnificent 35-year career. Born in the headquarters of French racing at Chantilly, Childs rode for King George V for 10 years until 1935. During the First World War, Childs served with the Royal Hussars and donated his riding fees to funds for fellow servicemen.

RIGHT: Windsor Lad was ridden by Charlie Smirke, arguably the greatest flat jockey never to be Champion Jockey. His early career suffered when he was banned for five years – "warned off", as the parlance goes – after his mount Welcome Gift was left at the post at Gatwick in 1928. The horse was later found to have problems starting while racing in India, indicating Smirke's innocence. Returning to the saddle, he excelled, particularly riding for the Aga Khan, and won the Derby four times. Smirke's victory aboard Tulyar in 1952 led him to joke, "What did I Tul Yar?"

A working-class man who grew up in inner London, Smirke was hugely popular with the capital's racegoers, and the feeling was mutual. An apocryphal story has it that in 1958, prior to the Derby, Smirke gave a nod and a wink to punters by pulling the tail of his ride Hard Ridden, indicating he fancied it to win, which it duly did.

Golden Boy

"God on four legs" was how journalist Sidney Galfrey described Golden Miller. The horse's achievements in winning the Cheltenham Gold Cup five times in succession between 1932 and 1936 were good enough to earn him legend status, but his victory in the 1934 Grand National turned him into a phenomenon. Winning both the National and the Gold Cup in the same year was unprecedented, and is a feat still unequalled.

Golden Miller might even have won the Gold Cup six times in a row, had bad weather not stopped the running of the race in 1937. His owner Dorothy Paget (pictured, below) was notoriously capricious in her choices and switched trainers, yet together horse and owner produced some of the finest National Hunt memories.

ABOVE: Golden Miller (left) at his stables and in his dotage.

LEFT: The 6–1 favourite Hyperion wins the Derby in 1933. This popular horse was a diminutive 15 hands high but was full of character and charm, and reputedly liked to stare at aeroplanes in flight. He was prodigious at stud, with a wide-ranging and successful progeny.

BELOW: Battleship was another horse small in stature but big in heart. The American-owned 11-year-old – who went on to have a brief stallion career – won a thrilling Grand National in 1938, piloted to victory by 17-year-old Bruce Hobbs, the youngest jockey to win the big race.

On a 1938 holiday to Switzerland, Champion Jockey Gordon Richards tried a spot of curling. Richards was joined on the trip to St Moritz by the famous owners and fellow jockeys of the day, including Steve Donoghue.

Richards was also a dab hand on the golf course. In 1937, he teed off at a chilly-looking Romford.

ABOVE: In a scene repeated through the war years, American soldiers enjoyed a picnic with their English girlfriends, on this occasion during a summer's day out to watch the Derby in 1943.

Two winners from this period merit highlighting. Airborne won the Derby in 1946, while My Love triumphed two years later. The story goes that romantically inclined wives and girlfriends bet in big numbers on both horses, the former for its links with paratroopers and the latter amid the demob joy of peacetime. Whatever the truth, the bookies are said to have taken a big hit.

ABOVE: While Gordon Richards dominated racing, young apprentice jockeys aspired to follow in the great man's stirrups. By 1944, 15-year-old Denis Dillon had finished second in both legs of the "autumn double", in the Cambridgeshire and in the Cesarewitch at Newmarket.

RIGHT: Part of Dillon's apprenticeship was to muck in with the mucking out.

The eventual winner, rank outsider Russian Hero at 66–1, leads over Becher's Brook in the 1949 Grand National.

ABOVE: Hail the conquering Russian Hero.

BELOW: Ever the most gruelling of races, the National was and remains the most arduous test for man and horse. Groggy jockey R Curran was helped by ambulance men after falling from Ulster Monarch in 1949.

As racing returned to some kind of normality, the fashionable set returned to place a bet at the 1949 St Leger at Doncaster.

ABOVE: Jockey J Power clung on admirably to his horse Bruno II in the St Helens Chase at Haydock in November 1949.

LEFT: Derby Day betting activity via the telephone in 1949.

Early morning, and riding into the sun, horses from Jack Waugh's Buckinghamshire stable are exercised on the gallops. Exemplifying the beauty of top racehorses in full flight were Star King (far left) and Master Venture (second left).

Courses for HORSES

Racecourses have been a part of the British landscape for centuries, whether through their great expanses of turf blending with rural surroundings, or their stands becoming an integral part of a more urban environment. While 60 have survived into the modern era, many have come and gone – 90 disappeared in the 20th century alone. Here are some of those lost, and historical scenes from those sites that have lasted the course.

Glorious Goodwood, as seen from the air in this stunning image from 1923.

Alexandra Park was more synonymous with the grand municipal palace in north London that loomed above it, but the racecourse had its own fame. It first hosted racing in 1868, and with a "frying-pan"-shaped course full of twists, turns and obstructed views, it was highly distinctive. It could hold races only over three distances – five furlongs,

ABOVE: Fred Winter, on Spaniards Close, lines up against Goa, ridden by Lester Piggott, at a 1962 Alexandra Park meeting.

one mile, and one mile and five furlongs.

While "Ally Pally" was popular in terms of attendance, thanks to a location within easy reach of millions, and especially successful for evening meetings, jockeys were not among the track's fans. Willie Carson even wished it was bombed. The course closed in 1970.

ABOVE: Long before the roar of jet engines, Gatwick echoed to the sound of thunderous hooves. Opened in 1891, the course was set up to replace the old Waddon track in Croydon. Served by its own railway station, Gatwick was a successful venue, and even hosted the relocated Grand National during the First World War. It continued to function up to 1940 (as this picture of the 1925 Horley Hurdle shows), but with another conflict demanding use of the land for an airfield, its days were numbered.

Sussex used to boast a feast of summer racing when back-to-back meetings were held at Goodwood, Brighton, and the now-defunct Lewes course. Perched on a ridge on the South Downs, Lewes had a long, if not always glorious, history. It was formally founded in 1727 (though racing had probably taken place well before that time), and enjoyed the patronage of the Prince Regent in its heyday.

By the 1930s it had a less savoury reputation and attracted the infamous razor gangs that plagued courses and were involved in organized protection and betting rackets. One major fracas in 1936 led to jail terms handed out to 16 men (including one by the name of Bert Blitz) involved in a long-running feud with roots in the criminal underworld of London.

Lewes' location and its rudimentary facilities meant that, once off-course betting became legal in 1961, its appeal dwindled, and it was closed in 1964 as part of the Horserace Betting Levy Board's reorganization of funding support for British courses. Modern-day trainers still use Lewes' gallops, however.

> *"The racecourse, with its commodious stand, is justly regarded as one of the finest in England."*
>
> – *The History and Antiquities of Lewes*, 1824

ABOVE & BELOW: Crowds gather for the last day of Lewes racing on 14th September 1964.

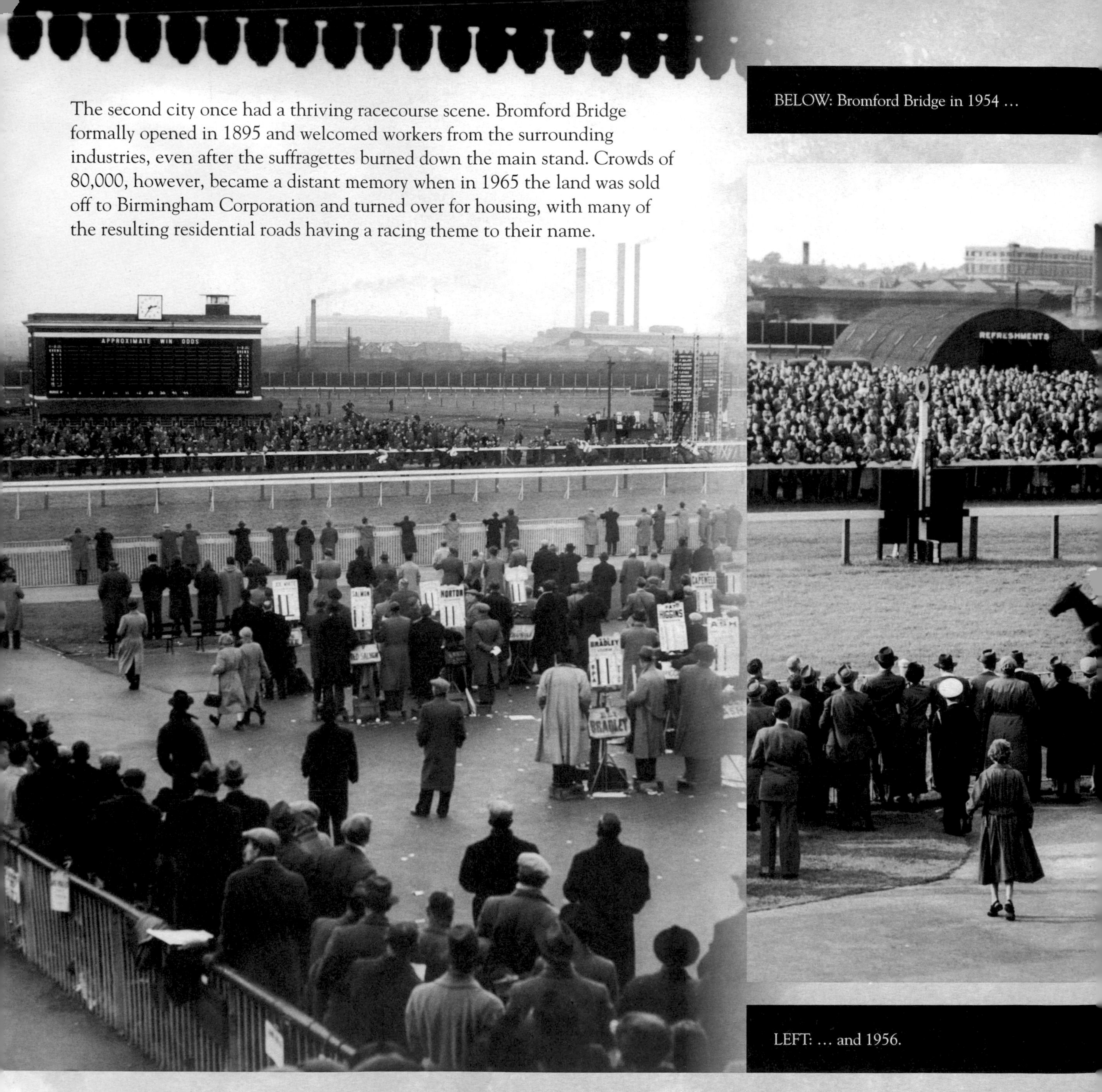

The second city once had a thriving racecourse scene. Bromford Bridge formally opened in 1895 and welcomed workers from the surrounding industries, even after the suffragettes burned down the main stand. Crowds of 80,000, however, became a distant memory when in 1965 the land was sold off to Birmingham Corporation and turned over for housing, with many of the resulting residential roads having a racing theme to their name.

BELOW: Bromford Bridge in 1954 …

LEFT: … and 1956.

ABOVE: A waterlogged Shirley Park in the south of Birmingham in 1951. By that time the course had been turned over for pony races. As a racecourse, it had thrived between 1899 and 1947. A golf course now occupies the site.

Racing in Manchester can be traced back to 1647, but a formally laid out venue had a peripatetic existence, switching location a number of times in the Salford area. The final site was a right-hander in Castle Irwell from 1902 until 1963. Yet again, financial pressures forced the course's closure and with it the end to a long tradition: Manchester held the final big race of the flat season, the November Handicap, which thereafter was switched to Doncaster.

ABOVE & LEFT: The melancholy scene on the last day of Mancunian racing, shortly before the goodbye Consolation Plate in November 1963.

ABOVE: Manchester race track in 1960.

LEFT: Track staff complete their work on the final day.

Racing in Lincoln had an even longer heritage than in Manchester, with some form of competition beginning in 1597. A proper course was established in 1773, with the March meeting and the Lincoln Handicap the curtain-raiser for the flat season. Once Lincoln ran into a post-war slump with a lack of quality runners, the course was doomed; it closed in 1964, though the Lincoln Handicap lives on at Doncaster and the grandstand building remains.

LEFT: Opening day for the last time at Lincoln.

Thankfully, many of the sport's best courses have survived – and few are finer than Goodwood. Set in the stunning downland of West Sussex, it is widely regarded by aficionados as the most beautiful course in racing, as well as one that plays host to top-drawer racing in the Glorious Goodwood meet.

Laid out in 1801 by the third Duke of Richmond, it has a testing right-hand course with numerous dips and inclines. But it is the vistas it provides that play a large part in drawing such a devoted following, together with a relaxing atmosphere.

ABOVE: With the Downs in the background, Scobie Breasley steers Hambleden to victory at Goodwood in the 1966 Richmond Stakes.

LEFT & ABOVE: Glorious scenes at Goodwood in the blazing heat of July 1961…

RIGHT: … though the British weather cannot *always* be guaranteed, as in 1966.

Bird's-eye views of two of Britain's finest courses. Newmarket, the home of flat racing, was pictured in all its splendour on Cambridgeshire Day in 1922 (above). While Epsom (right) might not have the social cachet of Ascot, nor the official status of Newmarket, it has earned a renown and special appeal all its own. As this 1928 shot of the Derby shows, the sheer scale of its premier event and the crowds it has attracted are vast. Today, the Derby still draws the biggest attendance in Britain for any single sporting event.

Knights of Racing's Realm
THE 1950s

A jockey takes a fall amid the muck, mayhem and magic of the Cheltenham Gold Cup in 1955.

As racing entered the television age and the post-war boom, the popularity of the sport grew, with yearly attendance figures in excess of 6 million. Racegoers were drawn to see some of the best horses and jockeys both on the flat and over the jumps, such as the Italian-trained Ribot, who was unbeaten in 16 races – including two wins in the Arc and one in the King George at Ascot – and is widely regarded as the best horse ever to come out of his country.

In **1950** a familiar British crowd favourite was still producing the goods: Gordon Richards rode his 4,000th winner the day before his 46th birthday. The Grand National of **1951**, meanwhile, saw only three of the 36 runners complete the race.

A **1952** dispute between the BBC and Tophams Ltd, the owners of Aintree, led to a Grand National radio row, eventually resolved when Tophams provided their own commentators, only for them to mistakenly announce that Teal – who was actually the winner – had fallen at the first fence. In **1953** Champion Jockey Sir Gordon Richards, after 27 unsuccessful attempts, finally won the Derby aboard Pinza. The year **1954** was the midway point for trainer Vincent O'Brien's magnificent sequence of three successive victories in the Grand National, while the famed Meld completed the fillies' Triple Crown with an impressive win of the **1955** St Leger. To cement her fame, she went on to be the dam of 1966 Derby winner Charlottown.

Arguably the most famous story of the decade came in **1956**. Poised to win the Grand National for his owner the Queen Mother, Devon Loch mysteriously sprawled and fell on to his belly within sight of the finishing post. That same year, for the first time since its foundation, no British-trained horse finished in the first three of the Derby.

In **1957** Aga Khan, the pre-eminent breeder and trainer of his era, died at the age of 80. Ballymoss became the most successful horse to date in terms of prize money when his victory in the Prix de l'Arc de Triomphe in **1958** took his winnings to £98,650. Tragedy struck in **1959** when top flat jockey Manny Mercer was killed before the start of a race at Ascot, when he was unseated and then kicked by his horse, Priddy Fair. Racetracks in the old days, with such dangers as concrete posts, were more hazardous environments than they are today.

BELOW: Fred Winter works out on the Downs in July 1954.

Lincoln on Show

The Lincoln meeting in March was the traditional start to the flat season and a welcome date in the 1950s racing calendar. Lincoln racecourse closed in 1965 and the meeting moved to Doncaster (see pages 70–1).

LEFT: Course staff sorted through the names of the star jockeys (including Gordon Richards) in 1950.

RIGHT: Mothers and babies watched from the rail to assess the form and action.

BELOW: Families gathered expectantly to see the horses contesting the day's racing.

–LEGENDS–

Sir Gordon Richards

The first – and only – jockey to be knighted, Gordon Richards is viewed by many experts and aficionados as the greatest rider of all time. His record number of victories and long, almost uninterrupted, reign as Champion Jockey, provides proof of his excellence. Richards won the honour an extraordinary 26 times, albeit in a time when jockeys didn't have to undertake quite the volume of mounts they do today. But it is Richards' character that has also made him such an enduringly popular figure.

The son of a Shropshire miner, Richards' love for all things equine reputedly began with his early rides on pit ponies. Apprenticed to Martin Hartigan, under whom he met his hero Steve Donoghue, Richards rode his first winner in 1921, and became Champion Jockey for the first time in 1925. It was the start of a shining career in which the thoughtful, modest and highly popular Richards ruled the racing roost for over a generation. Raised as a Methodist, his reputation was spotless, and his trainers Thomas Hogg, Fred Darling and, after the Second World War, Noel Murless, could rely on a level of consistency no other jockey could match. In one astonishing sequence, Richards rode 12 winners in succession.

Yet the greatest prize, the Derby, eluded him. The story was to have the perfect ending, however. In the Coronation year of 1953, he received formal acknowledgement of his standing in public life with a knighthood. Just six days later, in his final attempt to land flat racing's Blue Riband, Richards rode Pinza to victory, defeating the Queen's horse, Aureole.

After an injury suffered the next season while riding the Queen's horse Abergeldie at Sandown, Richards called time on an outstanding riding career to enjoy a modestly successful period as first a trainer and then as racing manager for Lady Beaverbrook.

After 28 years of trying, Gordon Richards finally won the Derby, steering Pinza to victory in 1953. Here he is pictured being led in by owner Sir Victor Sassoon.

> *I can't remember ever being told how to ride. I just got on a pony's back and away I went.*
>
> – Gordon Richards

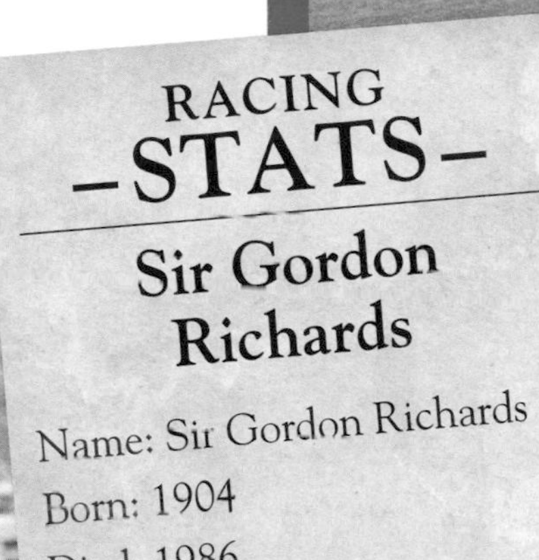

RACING –STATS–

Sir Gordon Richards

Name: Sir Gordon Richards

Born: 1904

Died: 1986

Races: 21,843

Wins: 4,870

Highlights: Derby winner 1953; winner of 14 Classics; Champion Jockey 26 times

ABOVE: The Epsom crowd roared the popular Richards over the finishing line.

BELOW: After witnessing Richards defeating her own horse, Aureole, the Queen, alongside Prince Philip, congratulated the knighted jockey on his victory.

Teal (left) jumps with Legal Joy on the way to a five-length victory in the 1952 Grand National. It was in this race that Aintree's amateur radio announcers had caused confusion when they declared that Teal had fallen at the first.

A policeman stands guard outside Aintree's New Yard stables ahead of the big race in 1952.

LEFT: Before the 287th running of the Newmarket Town Plate, one competitor had some last-minute stitching on her boots. The race was a regular event run outside of the auspices of conventional racing, and was won in 1952 by Betty Richards, niece of Gordon, for the second successive year. Seventeen of the 18-strong field had female riders. Each of them was presented with a bucket of sausages, thanks to Mr Horace Hawes, who had won the race in 1945.

A Star is Born

While Gordon Richards was coming to the end of his career, a fresh new face looked set to challenge him as the country's leading jockey. Lester Piggott was just 14 when the decade began, yet by its end he was the pre-eminent rider of his and perhaps all generations. He won his first Derby in 1954, five months short of his 19th birthday, and would win it again three years later. The boy set to become popularly known as "the Long Fellow" had very much arrived.

LEFT: Piggott trod carefully after being released from hospital following an injury in 1951. His early career was certainly not uneventful – he received the first of his suspensions by the Jockey Club at the age of just 14.

RIGHT: A sporting Piggott took to waterskiing in 1954.

RIGHT: The 14-year-old Lester, with his father, Keith, at Lambourn, where the youngster lived until 1954. Keith had been a successful National Hunt jockey himself; he excelled as a trainer, and would go on to win the Grand National in 1963.

Scandal! French-bred and trained horses dominated British racing, with wins in up to a third of the Classics during the decade. One French horse that attracted the wrong kind of attention was Francasal. In a blast from racing's less-than-spotless past, the horse was replaced with a ringer – fellow French horse Santa Amaro – for the Spa Selling Stakes at Bath in July 1953. Huge bets totalling £3,500 were placed on the impostor horse just before the race. To prevent the bookmakers from relaying information on the betting patterns and covering their potential losses by cutting the odds, telephone wires from the course were cut.

"Francasal" romped home at 10–1, but suspicious authorities withheld payouts. The conspiracy was eventually exposed and, in October, two of the accused, Old Etonian Lieutenant Colonel Robert Dill (left) and bookie Harry Kateley (centre), appeared at Bow Street Magistrates' Court. At their Old Bailey trial four out of the five men, including Dill and Kateley, were convicted and imprisoned. Francasal and Santa Amaro were later put up for auction – the former for £168 while the latter fetched £420.

In 1957 Brighton police keep a wary eye for any miscreants at the seaside racecourse, once notorious for being plagued by organized crime. Note the constable's distinctive white helmet, a feature of the Brighton force until it was merged with the Sussex constabulary in 1968.

One of the most dramatic races in the sport's history came in the 1956 Grand National. Devon Loch, owned by the Queen Mother, had cleared the final fence and was just 55 yards from the winning post when, without any warning, the horse suddenly skidded, flopped and came to a halt. ESB strode past to win in extraordinary circumstances, leaving poor Devon Loch and his jockey Dick Francis unable to finish.

Francis received heartfelt condolences (below). He would retire a year later after a bad fall, and go on to become a prolific author and crime writer, with much of his work based around racing. The reason for Devon Loch's sudden choke has never been clear – one theory is that he mistook a patch of darker ground for a fence and tried to jump it. The horse was put down in 1963, but his legend lives on – to do a "Devon Loch" is synonymous with any dramatic sporting failure when victory is within grasp.

Over the last, and Devon Loch (right) looked set fair to win.

LEFT: A disconsolate Francis walked past the winning post.

To the victors, the Derby spoils. Charlie Smirke won his second Blue Riband of the 1950s (and his fourth and final Derby) in 1958 aboard Hard Ridden (below), and entered the winner's enclosure (right) as a popular champion whose rugged style endeared him to many. Lester Piggott also enjoyed two Derby victories, steering Never Say Die home in 1954 and then the fragile but supremely talented Crepello (below right) three years later.

GEO S ELLIOTT

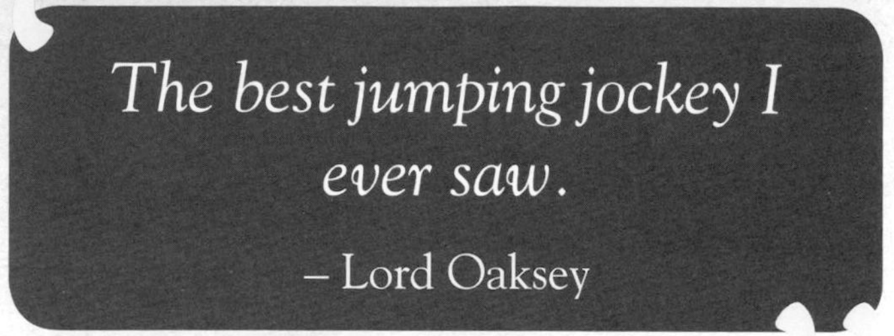

The supreme jump jockey in action in 1954, leading over the water at Newton Abbot.

RACING
–STATS–
Fred Winter

Name: Fred Winter
Born: 1926
Died: 2004
Wins: 923
Highlights: Grand National winner 1957, 1962; Cheltenham Gold Cup 1961–62; Champion Jockey four times

ABOVE: As a trainer, Winter gained wins with such famous horses as Lanzarote, Pendil and Crisp.

LEFT: Winter hobbled out from a London clinic after breaking his leg in December 1953.

–LEGENDS–

Fred Winter

Skill, determination, drive and pure guts: any champion National Hunt jockey requires these characteristics but few, if any, have had them in such abundance as Fred Winter. Winter excelled as both a trainer and a jockey, to make his indelible mark on the sport for half a century.

Apprenticed to his father, also called Fred, Winter tried his hand first of all on the flat, but his weight issues forced him to make the switch to the jumps in 1947. Early progress was halted when he broke his back in a fall at Wye. With his customary willpower and courage, Winter fought his way back to fitness and, after a year-long absence, was back in the saddle and winning races once more.

He landed the Grand National twice, riding Sundew in 1957 and then Kilmore in 1962. Gold Cup victories were collected in successive seasons from 1961–62, with the first of his riding championships coming in 1952–53, and three more to follow. But what many regard as Winter's finest performance came in the 1962 Grand Steeple-Chase de Paris. Riding Mandarin over the punishing figure-of-eight track at Auteuil, Winter had to contend with a broken bit and hence redundant reins, relying on sheer bodily strength to steer and cajole Mandarin around the course. The horse took inspiration from his rider, battling on despite injuring one of his forelegs. Summoning every ounce of energy, effort and courage, man and beast crossed the line to win by a head. It was horsemanship of heroic proportions and ranks as one of the greatest ever riding performances.

Winter would go on to win eight championships and two Nationals as a trainer, continuing to record victories right up until retirement in 1988, when he suffered a bad fall and was confined to a wheelchair. It was the end of one of racing's most glorious careers.

Fred Winter married Diana Pearson in May 1956, in racing's wedding of the year.

To mark Winter's retirement as a jockey in 1964, the Variety Club of Great Britain laid on a lavish luncheon at the Savoy, complete with suitably attired glamour girls.

Fifties Racing Faces

LEFT: The little and large show: South African boxer Ewart Potgieter, standing 7ft 2in shook hands with jockey G McComb at Brighton in 1955. Potgieter was reputed to be the second tallest boxer in history.

BELOW: Group Captain Peter Townsend found undeserved notoriety in the early 1950s for his relationship with Princess Margaret. Away from wooing an heir to the throne (as a divorcee, he was prevented from marrying Margaret), Townsend was a highly decorated veteran of the Second World War and a keen "gentleman" rider. In 1955 he weighed in for a race at Le Touquet in France.

Hollywood's blonde bombshell Jayne Mansfield presented the Variety Club of Great Britain trophy to a noticeably impressed jockey George Moore at a special charity event at Sandown in 1959.

Racing's Swinging Decade

THE 1960s

No sweat … National Hunt jockey Terry Biddlecombe takes it easy in his special sweat box in November 1964. One of racing's great characters, with a larger-than-life appetite for fun both on and off the track, Biddlecombe was billed as racing's "Beatle". At 23 he was, according to the *Daily Mirror*'s Bob Rodney, "the type for today. He's a laughing, unassuming country boy, from Upleadon (Glos.) with masses of curly hair. A blond Beatle. 'All I need is a guitar,' he grins."

Biddlecombe was no mere playboy, however. He was a Champion Jockey for three years, and rode over 900 winners, including in the 1967 Cheltenham Gold Cup. Today, Biddlecombe is best known as the husband of Henrietta Knight, trainer of three-times Cheltenham Gold Cup winner Best Mate.

Reflecting the huge shifts taking place in British society, horse racing underwent significant change in the 1960s. As a symbol of the Establishment, the sport and its age-old traditions might have sat at odds with the sweeping and dramatic transformations in an era of technological revolution and social upheaval. But while racing retained many of its fundamentals, it also moved with the times.

In **1960** the Grand National was televised for the first time, becoming the housewives choice for a yearly flutter. The same year the patrol camera was introduced. Gambling itself was revolutionized in **1961**, when off-course betting was legalized, and the high street betting shop was born, dramatically increasing betting turnover.

The **1962** Derby was more of a demolition derby after seven horses, including the favourite, Hethersett, fell after a collision on the hill down to Tattenham Corner. In **1963** Scobie Breasley completed a hat-trick of Champion Jockey titles, before, in **1964**, in one of the most eagerly anticipated of all showdowns, Arkle defeated Mill House to win an epic Cheltenham Gold Cup.

Starting stalls were introduced in **1965**, and in the same year came Sea Bird II's era-defining double in the Derby and the Prix de l'Arc de Triomphe. A court case forced the Jockey Club to grant training licences to women in **1966**, while a 10 per cent off-course betting tax was introduced. Foinavon made his unforgettable mark on racing history with his unlikely win after a monumental pile-up at the 23rd fence in the infamous **1967** Grand National, and the Jockey Club and the National Hunt Committee joined forces to create one overall body in **1968**.

Ten years after the death of Manny Mercer, flat jockey Derek Stansfield died after a fall at Hamilton in **1969**.

Thrilling action from the 1969 Grand National, with eventual winner Highland Wedding (far left) leaping over the fearsome Becher's Brook. Andrew Parker Bowles, former husband of Camilla Parker Bowles, is at the rear, riding Fossa. Former cavalry officer Parker Bowles rode with a tin plate in his back, courtesy of an earlier riding injury.

"The game ain't what it used to be."

– William "Digger" Hanley, street bookmaker

Gambling was one area of horse racing that experienced significant change. The days of street bookmakers like William "Digger" Hanley (left) of Hoxton in East London, were coming to an end, as off-course betting was legalized following the passing of the Betting and Gaming Act in 1961.

From May that year, betting shops could open (below) and were soon doing a brisk trade. On-course betting survived, but the times they were a-changing: female bookies gathered a crowd at Uttoxeter in 1967 (right), while Gus Demmy relied on some imaginative marketing when he dressed his staff as pearly kings and queens at his shop in Brazennose Street in Manchester (below right), leaving one old punter bemused.

J.A BIRCH
B.P.A
HAPPY JACK
HELLO DOLLY DARLING
SICILIAN LAD
STEALTHY APPROACH
VINDICATED
EPSOM
4 SINGER
5 ROXBURGH
EPSOM
2 WHISTLING FOOL
SP
BETTING SLIPS

–LEGENDS–

Arthur "Scobie" Breasley

Scobie Breasley had made his name in his native Australia and was 36 before he was tempted by J V Rank (brother of film magnate J Arthur) to ride in the UK. British racegoers were to enjoy a near two-decade treat in seeing a consummate racing artist in action.

Breasley oozed style and class for the way he rode, qualities that won him the admiration of his fellow jockeys, as well as making punters, trainers and owners happy. He used the whip sparingly, relying instead on his balance, poise and deft control to get the best out of his mounts. But Breasley was also courageous, a characteristic never better illustrated than when he was injured in a terrible fall at Alexandra Park in 1954. Despite a fractured skull that rendered him temporarily cross-eyed and with a loss of balance, he fought his way back to fitness and within three years was Champion Jockey.

Breasley won the Arc on Ballymoss in 1958 to confirm his re-emergence as a star of the flat, but he had to wait until his half-century before he landed the greatest prize, winning the Derby on Santa Claus in 1964. Breasley followed this up with a second win two years later on Charlottown. They were popular victories for a real gentleman of the sport. Dropping out of the saddle for good in 1968, Breasley trained in the UK, France, the US and Barbados, before eventually retiring full time and moving back home to Australia in 1990.

RIGHT: Ho, Ho, Ho: Breasley wins the 1964 Derby aboard Santa Claus.

ABOVE: It's off to work we go … In 1967 Breasley set off for Doncaster races, walking past a bevy of luxury vehicles.

BELOW: Breasley was a brave jockey and no stranger to the stretcher. After a fall at Brighton in June 1959, the Aussie hero arrived at a London clinic for treatment.

RACING
-STATS-
Arthur Breasley

Name: Arthur "Scobie" Breasley
Born: 1914
Died: 2006
Races: 9,716
Wins: 2,160
Highlights: Two Derby winners; Prix de l'Arc de Triomphe

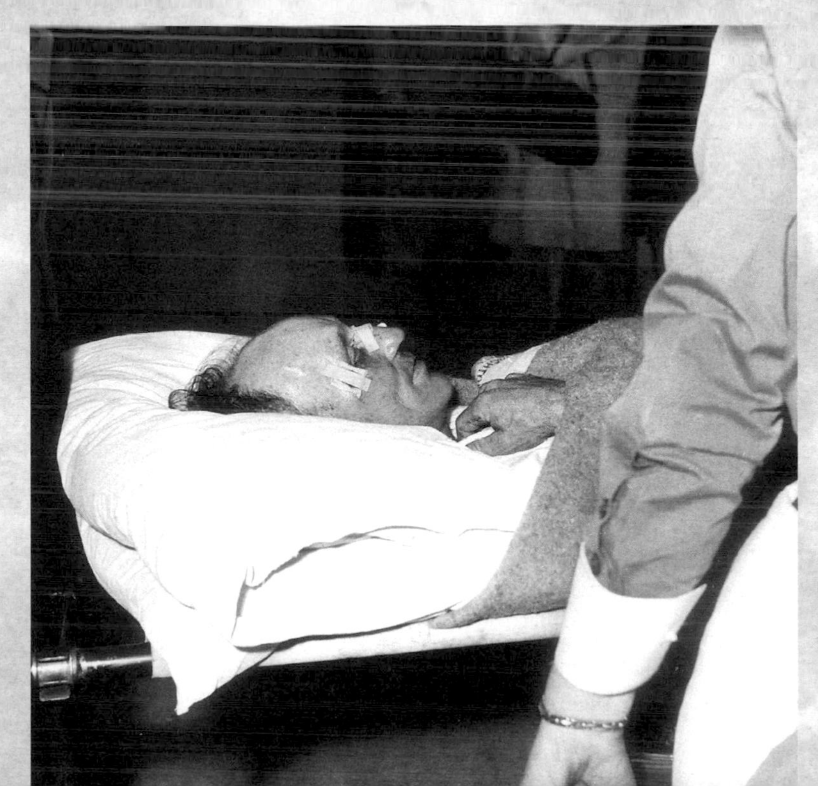

11

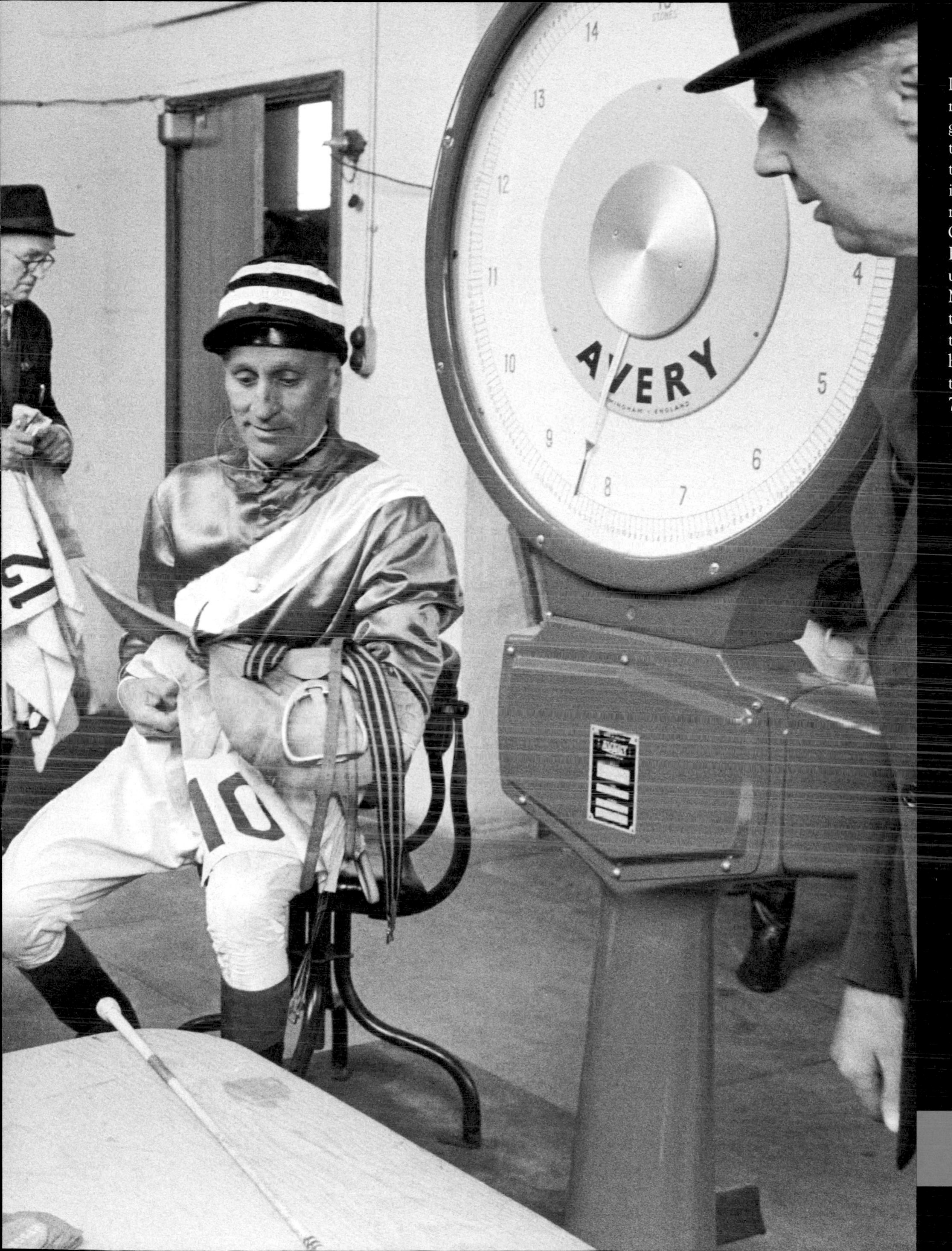

LEFT: In a timeless scene repeated away from the glare of the racing crowd, two jockeys went through the required procedure in the Epsom weighing room in April 1961. Champion Jockey Scobie Breasley registered just under 8½st, with Sammy Millbanks waiting his turn. Millbanks was one of those jockeys able to keep his weight down to the then minimum weight of 7st 7lb.

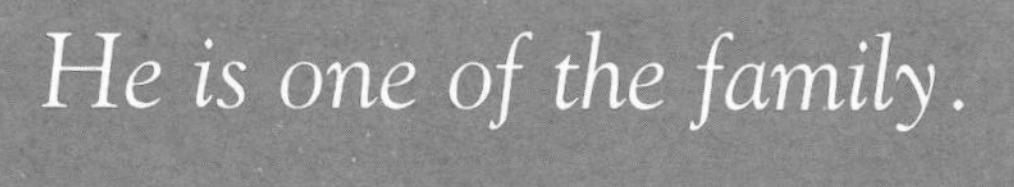

> *He is one of the family.*
>
> – the Duchess of Westminster

Pat Taaffe with Arkle and his owner, the Duchess of Westminster, after victory in the Cheltenham Gold Cup in 1966. The Duchess refused to let Arkle run in the Grand National, preferring to spare him the rigours of what was often a lethal race "because I adore him".

RACING
–STATS–
Arkle

Name: Arkle
Born: 1957
Died: 1970
Races: 35
Wins: 27
Highlights: Cheltenham Gold Cup 1964–66; Hennessy Gold Cup 1964–65

ABOVE: Arkle's skeleton in the Irish Horse Museum.

BELOW: Arkle, with his leg in plaster, beside jockey Paddy Woods, after finishing second at Kempton in 1966.

–LEGENDS–

Arkle

Few horses have been as much loved as Arkle, the famous steeplechaser affectionately known in his Irish homeland and beyond as "Himself". His domination of the National Hunt during the mid-1960s elevated him to superstar status when he was at his racing peak, but his renown lived on well after he died. In 2004, Arkle topped the *Racing Post*'s readers' poll for the greatest ever horse.

For all his fame and achievement, Arkle boasted only a modest pedigree. But with the happy coincidence that occasionally creates sporting excellence, the unity of a great team helped turn the raw material of a brilliant natural performer into a champion. Trainer Tom Dreaper was trusted by an understanding owner, the Duchess of Westminster, to get the best out of her horse. Paired with jockey Pat Taaffe, the combination was all but unbeatable.

In a four-year period between 1962 and 1966, Arkle won 22 out of 26 races including a triple triumph: the Cheltenham Gold Cup and a Hennessy Gold Cup double. He won all seven of his races in 1962–63 and remained similarly invincible over five races in 1965–66. Confronting the challenge of the superb young chaser Mill House, he saw off his rival by a decisive five lengths in the 1964 Gold Cup, in one of the sport's definitive races, before increasing his superiority in subsequent meetings. Arkle was so far ahead of the opposition that the authorities had to introduce two forms of handicapping: one for when Arkle featured in a race, another for when he was absent.

His career came to an abrupt end in December 1966 when he broke a pedal bone in the King George VI at Kempton. There was to be no ignominious end, however. Arkle recovered and saw out a peaceful retirement in the Duchess' home in County Kildare.

ABOVE: After his injury at Kempton, Arkle convalesced with Nellie the donkey, in a barn at Bryanstown Farm. His leg was X-rayed each month by a vet, with the Duchess of Westminster keeping a close eye on her horse's recuperation.

BELOW: Champion horse turned sheep herder; with trainer Tom Dreaper at Kilsallaghan in County Meath, 1965.

Arkle in full flow with Pat Taaffe, winning the 1965 King George VI steeplechase at Kempton.

One of the more unlikely winners in the 1960s – indeed of all racing – was Foinavon. The 100–1 rank outsider was entered for the 1967 Grand National more in hope that he would survive the course than any expectation that he would win – neither his owner Cyril Watkins nor trainer John Kempton even attended the meet. Jockey John Buckingham stepped in at the last minute to take the mount and the pair set off at a leisurely place.

Fate then intervened. At the 23rd fence, one of the lowest on the course, the riderless Popham Down collided with Rutherfords. The knock-on effect was to bring down horse after horse. Amid the chaos, Buckingham marshalled Foinavon, who had been way adrift of the leaders, clear of the melee and on to an almost miraculous victory, just holding off Honey's End, whose jockey, Josh Gifford, had remounted. Only 18 of the 44 starters finished.

The bookies weren't the only ones happy with Foinavon's victory. Owner Cyril Watkins (left) and trainer John Kempton toasted the horse's success

LEFT: No race for old men? The 1968 Grand National featured 68-year-old American jockey Tim Durant, riding High Landie. Rider and horse managed to complete the race.

RIGHT: James McCartney, father of Paul, with his horse Drake's Drum at Chester races in 1964. James' famous son had bought the horse for his racing-loving dad for £1,050. In 1966 the pair were at Aintree to see Drake's Drum win the Hylton Plate at odds of 20–1. The horse was later retired to Paul's farm in Scotland.

Proving a Point

By the 1960s, point-to-point racing (or, as it's often more colloquially known, amateur steeplechasing) had been in existence for well over 200 years. Indeed, it could be argued it gave birth to steeplechasing, since races between hunting steeds from church spire to church spire – in other words, from "point to point" – lay at the heart of the National Hunt's origins.

Attracting amateur riders from county hunts, point-to-point had long been both a nursery ground and "retirement home" for horses and jockeys, and a much-cherished part of the racing calendar. In 1965, an enthusiastic crowd braved the conditions at Glamorgan's Penllyn Castle.

In 1969 Miss Gay Walker rode April Witch to victory at Glamorgan.

LEFT & ABOVE: The day before the 1965 Derby, Sea Bird II is put through his paces beside empty stands that would soon resound to deafening cheers for this supreme champion. The French horse ran only eight races in a short career, but won seven of them and finished second in the other. His victory at the Derby was followed by a breathtaking six-length victory in the Prix de l'Arc de Triomphe, leading some experts to rank him as the greatest flat horse of all time.

The Vincent O'Brien-trained Larkspur wins the 1962 Derby – a race notorious for the falls of seven horses near Tattenham Corner. Four jockeys were kept overnight in hospital, including Wally Swinburn, father of future Derby winner Walter.

RIGHT: Lester Piggott won the Derby twice in the 1960s, on St Paddy in 1960 and then on Sir Ivor in 1968. Of the famed Sir Ivor, Piggott told the *Guardian* that "he wasn't a mile-and-a-half horse but he had this terrific turn of foot".

Piggott would go on to success in Sir Ivor's American homeland later that year, winning the Washington International at a mud-bound Laurel Park. With a devastating turn of pace, the horse won by three-quarters of a length. Piggott was criticized by American commentators who favoured mounts that led from the front. Piggott offered wry appraisal: when asked after the race at what point he had expected to win, he answered "three weeks ago".

LEFT: A beaming Madame Dupré led her horse Relko into the Derby's winners' enclosure in 1963. The race was not without controversy and intrigue. Relko and six others in the race had subsequent dope tests, which disclosed the presence of substances other than "a normal nutrient" – findings that cast suspicion on the result. However, it was never properly ascertained as to what the mystery substances were, all the horses were eventually cleared, and the prize money, totalling £35,338, was awarded.

Racing behind the Scenes

ABOVE: A cleaner dusts off the weighing-in scales at Sandown in December 1967.

BELOW: CCTV was introduced at Goodwood in 1966.

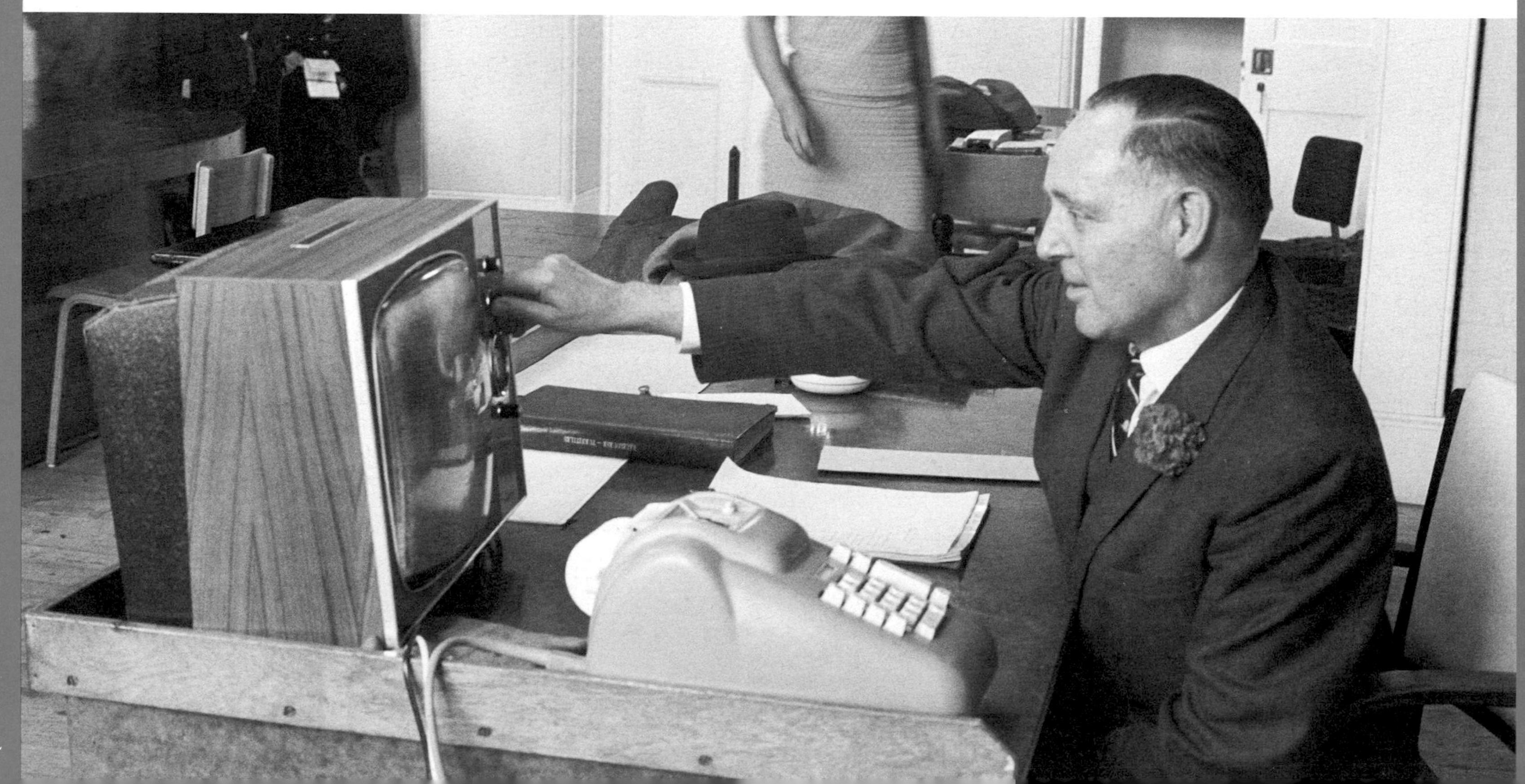

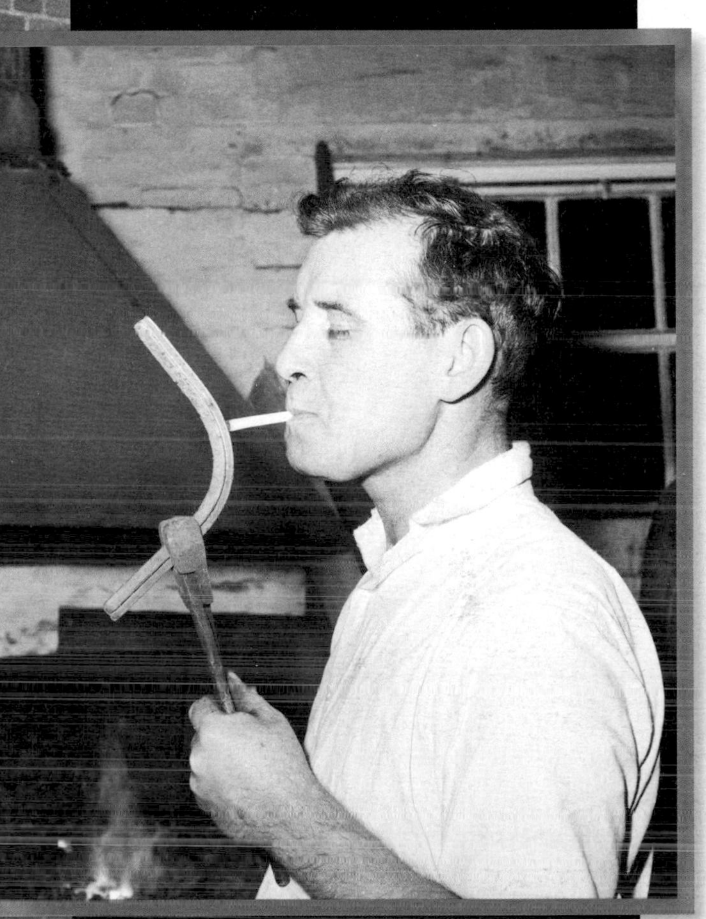

ABOVE: Taking a light from a glowing horseshoe at Newmarket's forge in 1964.

LEFT: Thumbs up as staff ready Sandown's huge Tote board.

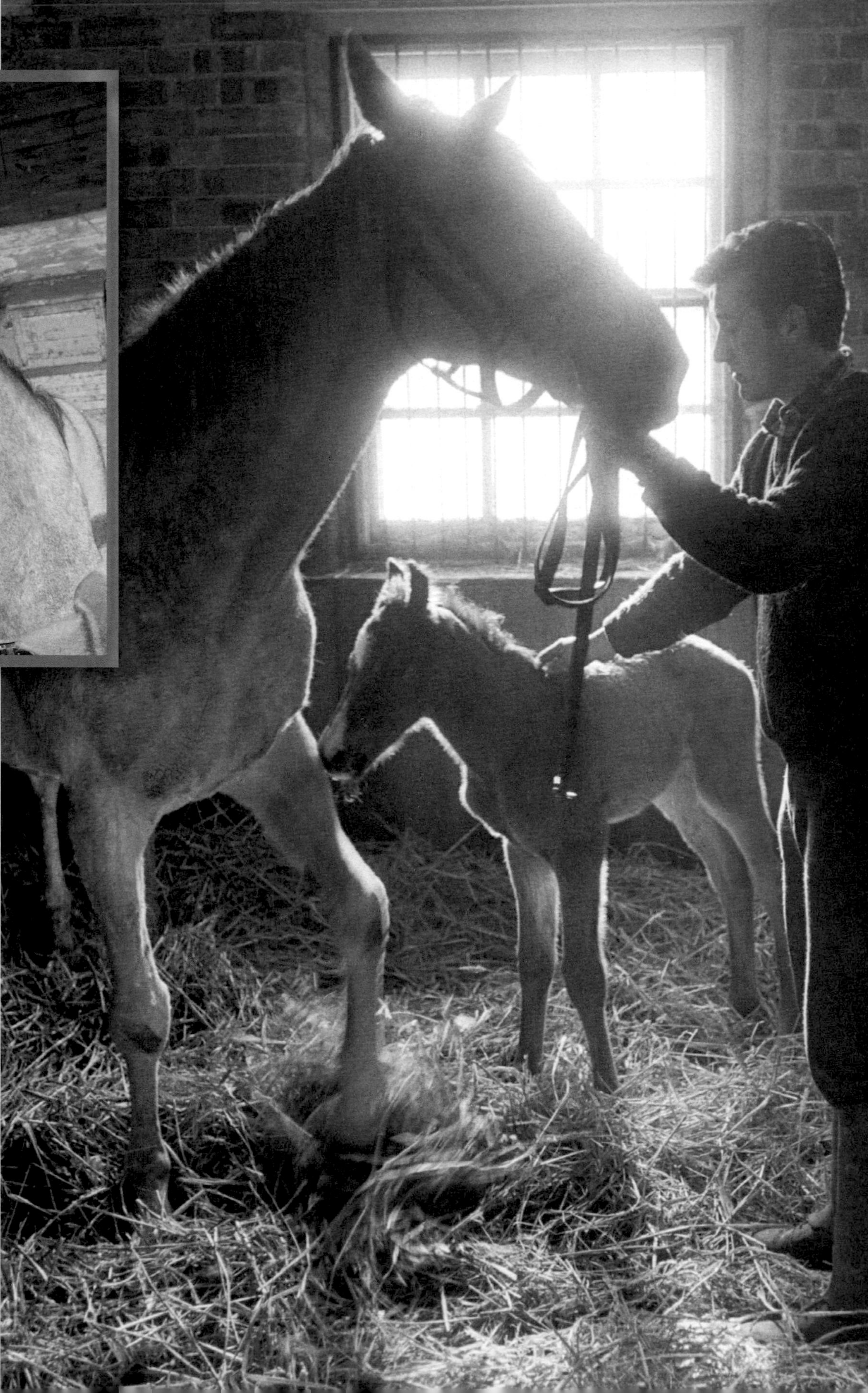

ABOVE: Horse dentist Archie Humble tends to one of his equine patients at Newmarket in 1964.

RIGHT: A beautiful scene at Newmarket in 1965. The National Stud had been located to the Suffolk town two years previously.

LEFT: Jockeys have always had to battle with their weight and, in 1969, Barry Brogan could only savour a modest breakfast. Brogan lived an eventful racing life; in his warts-and-all biography he confessed to accepting payments for tips, taking money to fix races, and a battle against alcoholism.

BELOW: National Hunt rider Ron Atkins was billed as the "mod" jockey with his taste for fashion and fast cars.

RIGHT: The business end … The buying, selling and breeding of horses has been as fundamental to its purpose as racing and gambling. Tattersalls had been auctioneers of thoroughbreds since 1745; in 1967, Vaguely Noble was paraded at Tattersalls' new sales ring, itself opened two years earlier. The horse, which would win the 1968 Arc, made headlines when he was sold for a world record of £136,000.

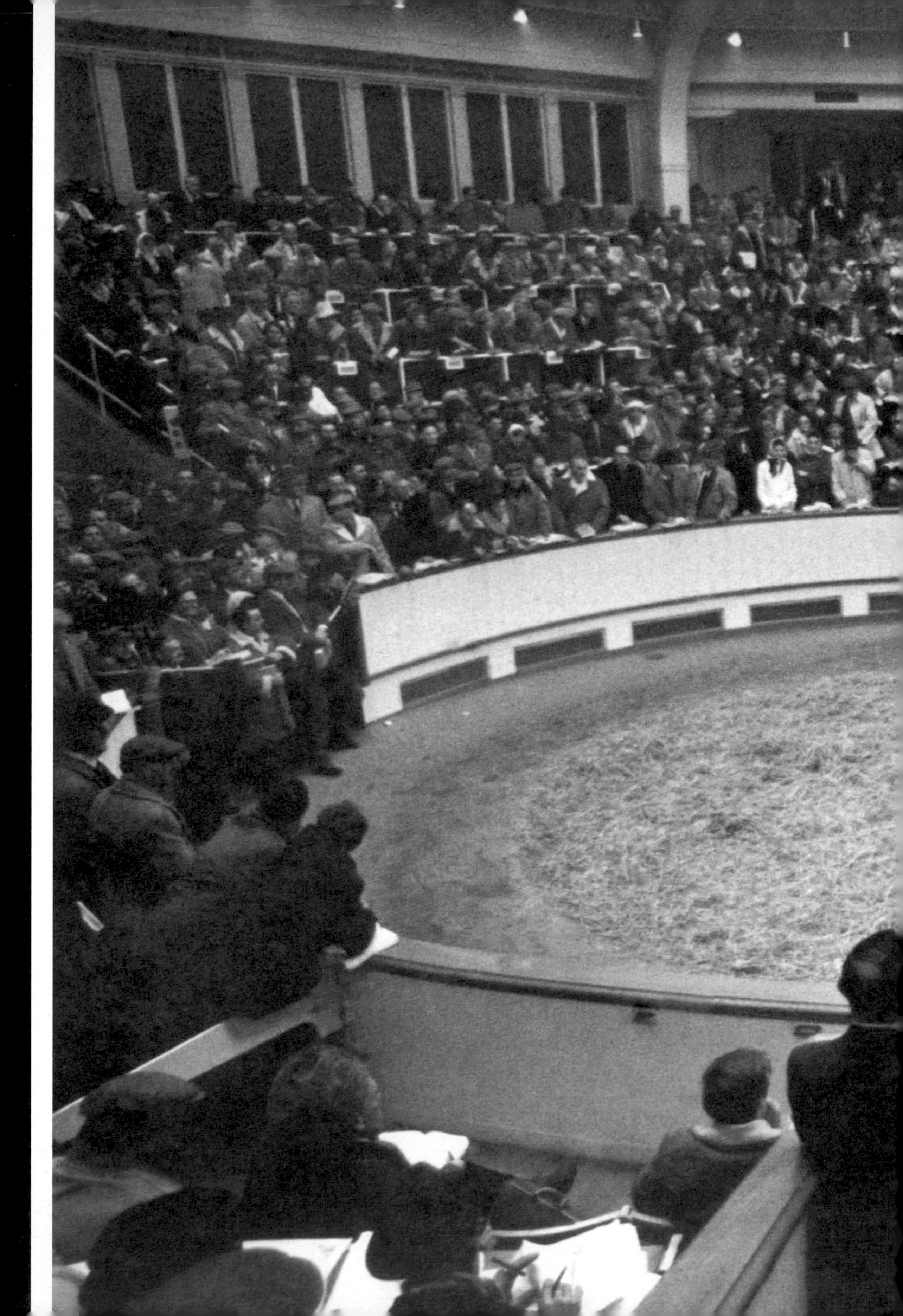

By Royal APPOINTMENTS

The roots of horse racing are embedded in the history of the Royal Family, particularly the Stuarts. James I effectively founded Newmarket as an equestrian centre, and Charles II actually rode in competition himself. The Rowley Mile course is named after Charles' nickname and the name of his favourite mount.

Queen Anne set up Ascot racecourse, still owned today by the Crown. Queen Victoria was said to disapprove of her son Bertie (later Edward VII) and his love of gambling on racing, though she was a keen spectator herself, and is reputed to have broken a window in the royal box at Ascot after she became so excited by the thrilling conclusion to one race. Successive kings, queens, princes and assorted royals have lent their patronage, and often active support, to racing. Not for nothing has racing long been dubbed the sport of kings …

Queen Elizabeth II and her racing manager Lord Porchester excitedly watch the finish of the 1978 Derby, won by Shirley Heights (see page 166). The Queen's own horse, English Harbour, languished in 18th place.

LEFT: Queen Elizabeth has been a dedicated horse-racing fan and owner almost her entire adult life. While she has not been able to land the biggest prize of all in the Derby, she has regularly won at Ascot, including a quartet of victories in 1957.

The winning streak included a superb triumph in the Oaks. A proud owner led the winning filly Carrozza and jockey Lester Piggott into the unsaddling enclosure.

BELOW: The Queen Mother was another royal who was an ardent racing follower. In 1973 at Newcastle she spoke to jockey Ron Barry after his victory in the 1973 Whitbread Gold Cup Handicap Chase, aboard Charlie Potheen.

Scenes from a Royal Scrapbook

ABOVE: Queen Mary and King George VI at Derby Day in 1937.
RIGHT: Princess Margaret at the National Hunt Ball in 1956.

ABOVE: Aintree 1956, and two generations of the monarchy, the Queen and her mother, talk to jockey Dick Francis, who rode for the latter for four years between 1953 and 1957.

RIGHT: The two Elizabeths at Cheltenham in 1957.

The Queen Mother was accompanied by her grandchildren, Princess Anne and Prince Charles, for a beautiful second day at Royal Ascot in 1980.

A rare trip to the rails for the then Princess Elizabeth and her mother in the 1951 Derby. The pair were joined by Lord Roseberry, to gain a close-up view of victory for another with royal "connections", Arctic Prince.

The royal box at Epsom has provided the best seats – and arguably the finest standing view – in racing. In 1961 (above) Queen Elizabeth looked decidedly more concerned than her mother, while it was a case of all eyes left at the 1993 meeting with her mother and eldest son.

Controversy arose in 1989 when the Queen's popular trainer, Major Dick Hern, was removed from the royal stables at West Ilsley. It caused widespread criticism; Hern was paralysed after breaking his neck in a fall in 1984 and suffered a heart attack four years later. Amid the furore, it was apparently all smiles when trainer and monarch met in July 1989.

No strangers to life in the saddle, the royals have in the past taken to galloping on various courses. In 1968 (below) at Ascot there was a competitive field of regal runners and riders including Queen Elizabeth, Prince Philip, the Duke and Duchess of Kent, Prince Charles, Princes Margaret and Lord Snowdon.

Charles took part in a more competitive race in 1980 (inset) when he partnered Allibar at Ludlow races. The duo came second in a 3-mile handicap chase for amateur riders.

5

The Queen celebrates another victory (though not for her own horse) at the 1988 Derby. Thirty-five years earlier, she witnessed her debut win when Choir Boy, a 100-to-6 shot, took the Royal Hunt Cup in 1953 (inset).

Champions All

THE 1970s

Stable lads and Donald "Ginger" McCain, trainer of Red Rum, celebrate with pints of Guinness to mark the horse's first Grand National win in 1973.

Famous horses, brilliant jockeys, memorable races – for many devotees, the 1970s represented a true golden age for racing. Horses like Nijinsky and particularly Red Rum ran their way into the nation's affections, capturing the imagination of both ardent racing fan and casual observer alike.

Nijinsky was the first to make his mark, winning the colts' Triple Crown in **1970**. A year later in **1971** Mill Reef won the Derby, the King George VI and Queen Elizabeth Stakes, and the Prix de l'Arc de Triomphe.

The year **1972** saw the Jockey Club allow flat races for female jockeys for the first time. That same year Mill Reef broke a leg, but was saved for stud. In **1973** handicapping was given another shake up, when it was agreed to have an organized system on a centralized basis providing computerized ratings. Before that, in a world a million miles away from the now highly centralized current set-up, horses could receive different weights for races in different parts of the country.

Gay Future's connections pulled off what looked like a stunning betting coup when the horse won a novice hurdle at Cartmel in August **1974**. The 15-length win at odds of 10–1 aroused suspicions, fuelled by the withdrawal of runners at other races that had been included in a large number of double and treble bets involving Gay Future. The bookies were vindicated at a later trial when the conspirators were found guilty of attempted fraud, though the sympathetic Judge Caulfield handed out relatively lenient fines. Also in **1974**, Linda Goodwill became the first woman to beat male jockeys when she won at Nottingham.

L'Escargot denied Red Rum a hat-trick of Grand National wins in **1975**, while in **1976** women were cleared to race under National Hunt rules. A year later, in **1977**, women could finally become members of the Jockey Club, after 225 years of waiting.

John Banks, the bookmaker who welcomed the legalization of high street betting shops in 1961 as "a licence to print money" was banned by the Jockey Club in **1978** for three years for breaches of rules on receiving confidential information. Banks described the ruling as coming from a "kangaroo court". The decade closed with a landmark victory in **1979**, as Troy won the 200th Derby in spectacular style.

Nijinsky exercising at Vincent O'Brien's Ballydoyle stables, in July 1970. O'Brien was phenomenally successful both over the jumps and on the flat, and the first trainer to install all-weather gallops.

–LEGENDS–

Nijinsky

Sharing a name with the great Russian ballet dancer, Nijinsky performed with similar virtuoso élan and flair. He ranked as one of the great flat horses of the modern age, thanks to becoming the first colt to win the Triple Crown since Bahram in 1935, and for his show-stealing speed and all-round class.

Nijinsky was a progeny of perhaps the greatest thoroughbred stallion of all time – Northern Dancer – and continued a line that has in large part defined modern racing. Nijinsky's five wins in his first season heralded something special: true greatness was set to spring from Vincent O'Brien's stable.

It was O'Brien who astutely spotted Nijinsky's potential, and his faith was rewarded in style in 1970. First Nijinsky took the 2000 Guineas, before a magnificent victory in the Derby. Under Lester Piggott's masterful control, the triumph represented man and horse in perfect harmony.

Victory in the St Leger completed the Triple Crown, but it was to be Nijinsky's last command performance. A bout of ringworm had taken its toll and defeats in the Arc and Champion Stakes by horses he would have beaten easily at his best spelt the end for a brief but wonderful career. "A horse is like a car: he has only a certain mileage," reasoned O'Brien, and his champion went on to enjoy a long and productive stud career, siring such famous names as Derby winners Golden Fleece, Shahrastani and Lammtarra – chips off the old block if ever there were.

"*The best thing I ever saw.*

– Charles Engelhard, Nijinsky's owner, on the 1970 Derby win"

RACING

–STATS–

Nijinsky

Name: Nijinsky
Born: 1967
Died: 1992
Races: 13
Wins: 11
Highlights: Triple Crown 1970

LEFT: Piggott and Nijinsky in victory, after the 1970 Derby.

BELOW: The pair went on to win at Ascot in the King George VI and Queen Elizabeth Stakes in July 1970.

Women were making inroads into the previously restricted world of horse racing, with a number of breakthrough rule changes to encourage greater female participation. In 1974, at the National Equestrian Centre in Stoneleigh, Warwickshire, seven young women apprentice jockeys had a breather during their six-week course. Those who made the grade could apply for a professional licence.

The presence of women in racing was still something of a novelty, however, and a group of female jockeys was a newsworthy photo opp. At a racing day at Brands Hatch in April 1974, Meriel Tufnell (in the driver's seat) was given a helping hand. Tufnell was the first woman to win a race after the Jockey Club relaxed the rules of races for female jockeys in 1972, when she won the Goya Stakes at Kempton Park, bringing home 50–1 mount Scorched Earth.

–LEGENDS–

Lester Piggott

Over a prodigious career that spanned six decades, Lester Piggott had such phenomenal success that any listing of his achievements cannot do his achievements justice. The bare facts are that he was one of the most prolific winning jockeys of all time, but they only hint at what made Piggott special. For many people, Piggott was simply the greatest flat jockey of all time

Piggott was born to race. He came from a family that had roots in the sport dating back to the 18th century. His grandfather Ernie had won a hat-trick of Grand Nationals and his father, Keith, was famed as both a jockey and trainer. His son was riding competitively from a tender age and bagged his first winner at 12; Piggott Jnr. barely looked back for nearly 40 years.

He was nicknamed "the Long Fellow" due to his height of 5ft 8in – tall for a flat jockey – and throughout his career he struggled to make the weight, but did so with success, providing testimony to his phenomenal determination. His physical sacrifices were rewarded with exceptional strength and fitness, and underpinned his glittering triumphs. Piggott rode such famous mounts as Nijinsky, Sir Ivor and The Minstrel to victory, and formed a formidable partnership with legendary trainer Vincent O'Brien. On occasion Piggott could draw on sheer brute force and willpower, as with his sixth Derby win aboard Roberto in 1972, when he virtually dragged the horse over the line to win by a nose.

A testament to Piggott's genius was his ability to get the very best out of horses that were not ranked as the finest. He combined perfect judgement of pace and a distinctive riding style with raw guts and often ruthless determination. Doubters spurned his talents at their peril: when odds-on favourite El Gran Senor finished second in the 1984 Derby, costing his owners millions in stud value, Piggott was reputed to say to the people who had chosen Pat Eddery as their jockey, "Do you miss me?"

During his career Piggott was a taciturn individual and earned a reputation for parsimony – he was jailed in 1987 for tax evasion – but while the scandal curtailed his career as a jockey and trainer, it did not diminish his standing as one of racing's true greats.

RACING –STATS–

Lester Piggott

Name: Lester Piggott
Born: 1935
Races: 21,000 (est.)
Wins: 4,493 (flat)
Highlights: Nine Derby winners; winner of 30 Classics; Champion Jockey 11 times

> *An iconoclast who became an icon.*
>
> – Sir Peter O'Sullevan

RIGHT: Piggott's bravery was unquestioned. Here he is pictured after sustaining head injuries in April 1981.

LEFT: The 12-year-old Piggott in familiar surroundings.

BELOW: At home playing horse with his daughter Maureen, while wife Susan held the baby of the family, Tracy.

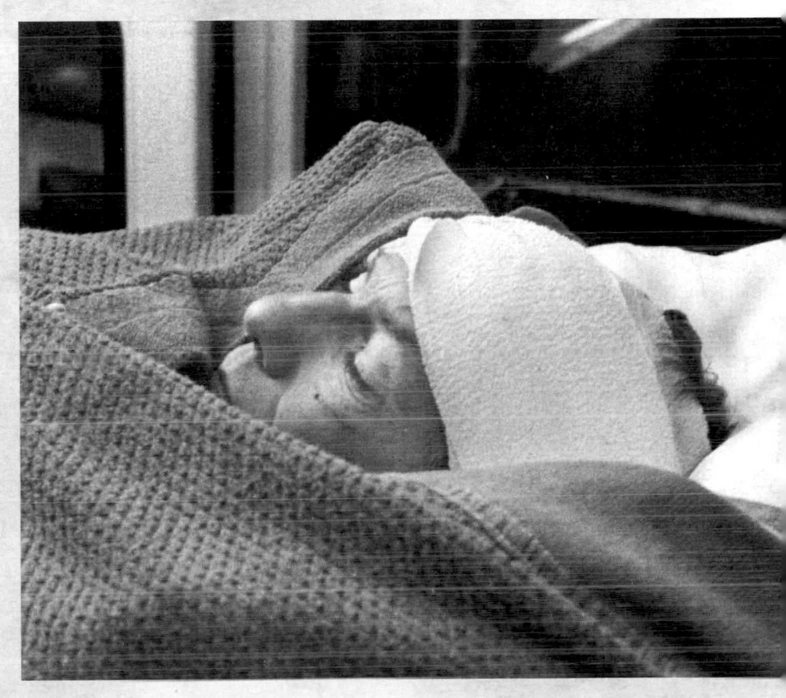

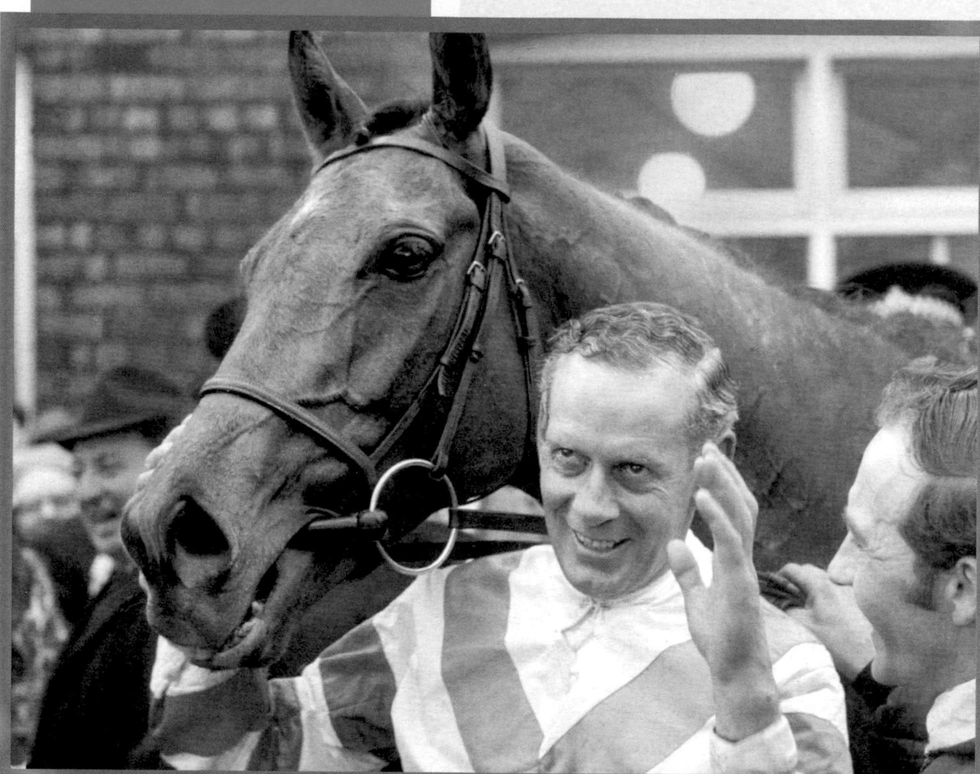

Veterans rally: Pat Taaffe (above), forever associated with the great Arkle, enjoyed a fine swansong to a wonderful career with victory in the 1970 Grand National, on Gay Trip. Riding at top weight, it was Taaffe's second win in the race, and came a full 15 years after his first.

Stan Mellor (right), meanwhile, rode to his 999th win, aboard Prairie Dog in the Tony Teacher Challenge Trophy Handicap Chase at Cheltenham in December 1971. Mellor became the first man to ride 1,000 National Hunt winners when he won with Ouzo at Nottingham later that month. Mellor ended his career in the saddle with 1,035 winners, and went on to become a successful trainer.

RIGHT: Brian Fletcher shows his son Andrew a painting of his father's famous ride on Red Rum in the 1973 Grand National. Fletcher won the big race twice with Red Rum but not the history-making third triumph in 1977, when Tommy Stack took the reins.

–LEGENDS–

Red Rum

No one would claim that Red Rum was the greatest ever jumps horse. Over a long National Hunt career (and 10 races on the flat) he would have struggled to compete at the Blue Riband events of the Cheltenham Gold Cup or the King George VI Chase. But at the Grand National, it was a different story. In winning the most testing of all races an extraordinary three times – as well as two seconds for good measure – Red Rum's achievement ensured his name will live on forever.

Few races and few racehorses have been so intertwined as "Rummy" and the National. Indeed, it could be argued that the horse saved the race: it had been struggling financially against its rivals, but Red Rum's captivating performances gave the meeting and its showcase race a new lease of life.

Red Rum's early career gave little hint of what was to come. He had been passed between various owners without making much of an impression. But in 1972 he was bought by Donald "Ginger" McCain, an idiosyncratic Merseyside taxi driver and trainer, on behalf of owner Noel le Mare. McCain put Red Rum through his paces on the Southport beaches, the seawater benefitting a horse that had suffered from acute lameness, and within a year he was ready for the 1973 National.

Red Rum's triumph in the race came after he hauled in the valiant Antipodean front-runner Crisp, who was carrying 23lbs more weight. The victory by three quarters of a length came in record-busting time, taking a remarkable 18 seconds off the previous mark. A year later, Red Rum carried top weight but repeated the feat, defeating another famed horse in L'Escargot. The latter gained revenge in 1975, and Rag Trade consigned Rummy to second place in 1976, but a year later, the nation's favourite pulled off a remarkable third win by a 25-length margin.

It was an extraordinary sequence of results, and such epic performances turned Red Rum into a sporting hero. In retirement he became a celebrity, opening shops and making regular TV appearances. He lived to the ripe old age of 30 and was buried, appropriately enough, by the winning post at Aintree.

RACING –STATS–

Red Rum

Name: Red Rum

Born: 1965

Died: 1995

Races: 110

Wins: 27

Highlights: Grand National 1973, 1974, 1977; Scottish National 1974

He was my friend. Given the choice between him and my wife, she'd have gone very quickly.

– Ginger McCain

Famous faces were always keen to be pictured alongside their fellow celebrity. Actress Amanda Barrie gave Rummy a brush down (above) while Liverpool's manager Bill Shankly paid a visit to McCain's yard to meet another local hero (below).

While opening a betting shop in Leamington Spa in 1982, Red Rum brought the town to a standstill.

LEFT: Red Rum made a show-stealing performance at the 1977 BBC Sports Personality of the Year awards.

BELOW LEFT: Over the fences and far away: Red Rum leaps to win at Aintree for the third time, this time ridden by Tommy Stack.

RIGHT: Out on his beloved Southport beach.

Lords of the Flat

Flat racing enjoyed its own golden age in the early 1970s with a succession of all-time greats. Mill Reef (below) vied with Nijinsky for acclaim, winning 12 out of 14 races, including a memorable trio in 1971 in the Derby, the King George VI and Queen Elizabeth Stakes (by a then record six lengths) and then, most famously, the Prix de l'Arc de Triomphe, becoming the first English-trained winner of the race for 23 years. A chipped cannon bone in his foreleg put paid to his racing career in August 1972, but he recovered (right, at trainer Ian Balding's stables) and went on to sire Derby winners Shirley Heights and Reference Point.

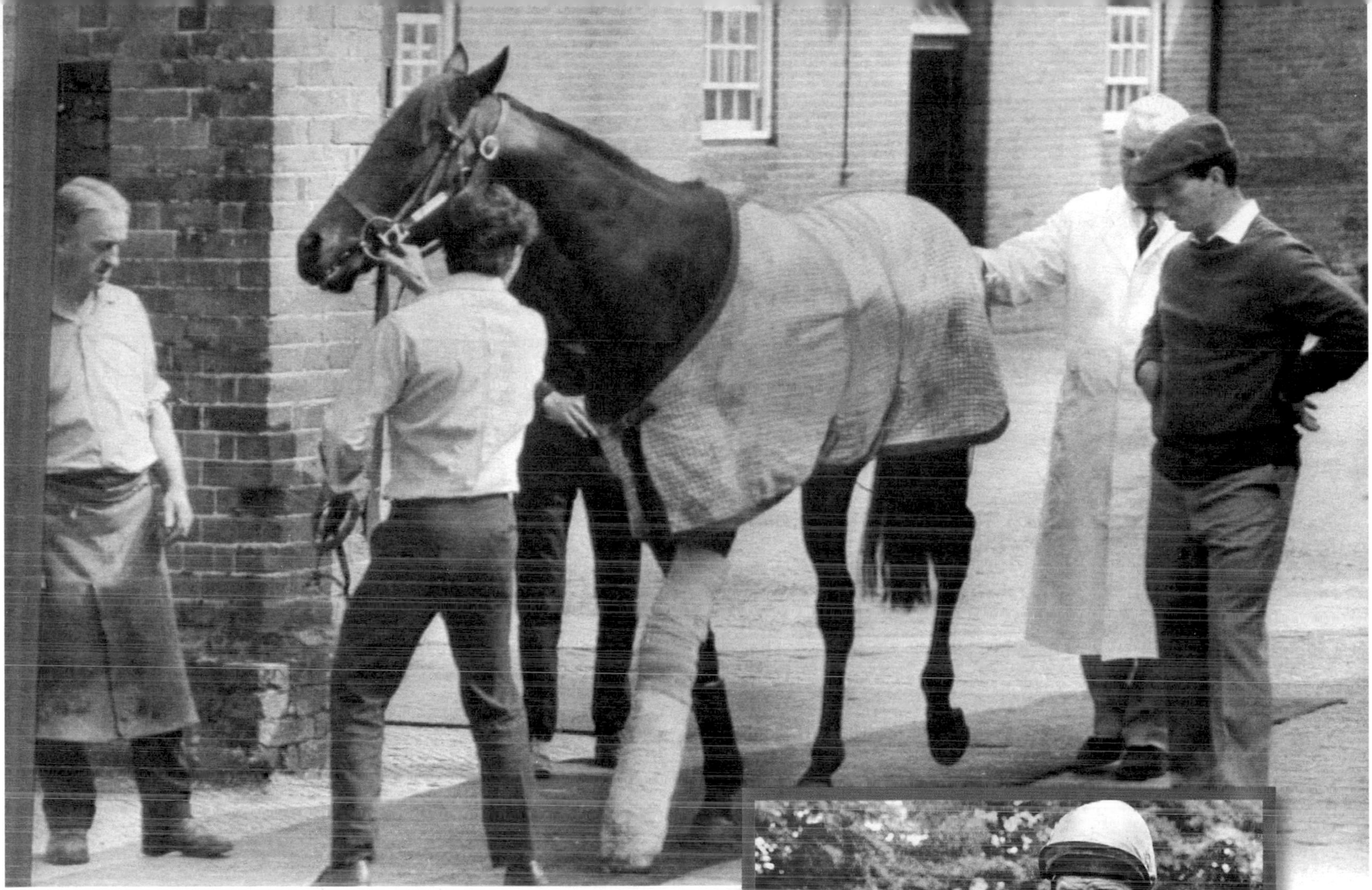

Brigadier Gerard was Mill Reef's contemporary rival. "The Brig" defeated Mill Reef in a famous 2000 Guineas in 1971, with a decisive win under Joe Mercer. The pair's other numerous big-race wins included the 1972 Eclipse Stakes (right), and provided welcome evidence that modest pedigree and ownership could still triumph in an increasingly commercial environment dominated by wealthy owners. Brigadier Gerard was bred from a mare who had never won a race and the husband-and-wife ownership team of John and Jean Hislop did not have the financial muscle of rival owners. But their horse lost just once in 18 races over a wide range of courses and distances, to become a true icon.

Stable life in the 1970s. Ocean King patiently allowed cat Jose to get comfortable on his back (above). In 1975, a "million-dollar trio" (inset) got to know one another at the Dunchurch Lodge Stud at Newmarket. The three foals were sired by world-renowned fathers: Mill Reef, Brigadier Gerard and My Swallow.

That same year at Newmarket there were some less happier racing protagonists (right). The course's stable lads had come out on strike to campaign for better pay in a trade that was notorious for its poor wages and conditions. Months of talks between the trainers and the Transport and General Workers Union had come to nothing, and the resulting dispute was a bitter one. While some jockeys were supportive, others, such as Lester Piggott, were less so, and even charged strikers at the starting gate as fights broke out between punters and pickets. Agreement between the lads and trainers was eventually reached, though 71 lads were sacked on their return to work.

> *It will always be an existence rather than a career.*
>
> – Willie Carson on life as a stable lad

Away from the glitz of race day, much of the hard graft in developing winning horses was done in training …

Nigel Angus' yard at Cree Lodge in Ayr. Angus had trained the giant Roman Warrior to win the Ayr Gold Cup in 1975.

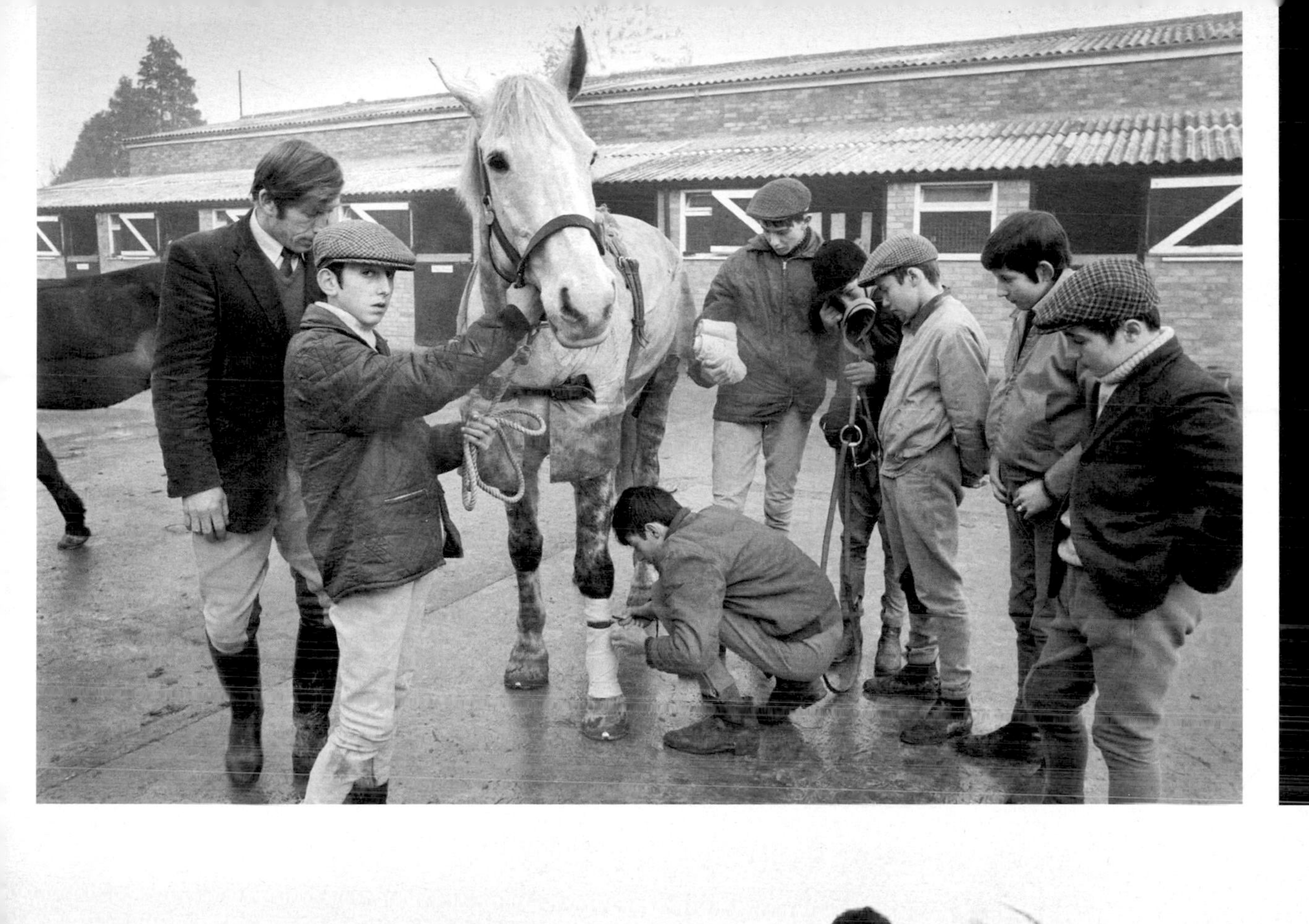

LEFT & BELOW: Scenes from the Apprentice Jockey Training Centre at Great Bookham in Surrey, 1970.

ABOVE: Shirley Heights wins a thrilling 1978 Derby. Jockey Greville Starkey ran down Hawaiian Sound in the last strides, and so prevented the great American jockey Willie Shoemaker, at the age of 46, from adding the English Blue Riband to his multiple American triumphs. Shirley Heights was the son of Mill Reef, and continued the winning lineage by siring Slip Anchor, who won the Derby in 1985.

RIGHT: At the 1979 pre-Derby Press Club dinner, Lester Piggott presented a salver to trainer John Dunlop (left), alongside actor Wilfred Hyde-White. Dunlop was training well into the 21st century, with over 3,500 winners setting out from his Arundel stables.

Not a man known for his conspicuous humour, Piggott was nonetheless willing to pose for the *Daily Mirror*'s Charlie Ley in 1978. "I won't fall off, will I?" he asked Ley with a smile.

Piggott still reigned supreme in the 1970s, illustrated by his eighth Derby victory in 1977 aboard The Minstrel (above). Other jockeys, however, were challenging for supremacy. Pat Eddery won the jockeys' championship four years running between 1974 and 1977, and triumphed in the Derby in 1975, riding Grundy (opposite top). New stars were also emerging, including American rider Steve Cauthen (right, sharing a tandem with the Long Fellow) and Willie Carson, who rode Troy to success in the "King George" in 1979 (opposite below). The pair had also won the Derby earlier that year.

globetrotter
globetrotter

All the queen's horses. At West Ilsley stables, Major Dick Hern presented the 13 horses he trained for the monarch. Left to right, back row: Star Harbour, Circlet, Alma, Tartan Pimpernel, Dunfermline, Mary Fitton. Front row: Valuation, Chain of Reasoning, Fife and Drum, Duke of Normandy, Rhyme Royal, Gregarious, Paintbrush. The filly Dunfermline was the Queen's most successful horse, winning the Oaks and St Leger in 1977.

Racing Characters, Crowds AND FACES

The rich, the ribald, the colourful, eccentric, famous and infamous – Britain's racecourses and the sport as a whole has attracted all manner of characters through the decades.

Prince Monolulu, the famous racecourse tipster, charms the Aintree crowd in 1953.

> *I gotta horse! I gotta horse! I gotta horse to beat the favour-ite!*
>
> – Prince Monolulu

Prince Monolulu was born Peter Carl McKay in 1881 on the Caribbean island of St Croix, and became one of the most famous and much-loved of all racecourse characters. With his distinctive colourful robes and feathered headdress, his regal persona enchanted and entertained the public on courses, in newsreels, and even on stage and in film, with his memorable "I gotta horse" catchphrase.

His story reads like an outlandish novel. Arriving in Britain in 1902, he joined the chorus of the West End show *In Dahomey* before working as a fortune-teller, musician, lion tamer and even a "cannibal" in a roadshow that travelled around the Continent. His association with racing began when he worked for an Irish tipster at the Derby in 1903, developing a distinct patter to drum up business.

After spending most of the First World War in a German internment camp he returned to the racetrack, developing his skills and honing his "I gotta horse" catchphrase, inspired by a religious revivalist called Gypsy Daniels. Legend has it that in 1920 Monolulu won the then vast sum of £8,000 on the Derby with a punt on the outsider Spion Kop. Whether true or not, it cemented his reputation as the tipster to follow, even if most of his bets never came in. Punters would offer him "silver" (often a sixpence) in return for a sealed envelope containing the name of his mystery tip.

Entertaining the crowds at Epsom in 1949 (above) and 1937 (left). The latter race was won by Mid-day Sun, owned by Mrs G B Miller, who became the first female owner to win the race.

Future Prime Minister Winston Churchill took his beloved wife Clementine to sample the atmosphere of Derby Day in 1923.

LEFT: "Old" Kate O'Neill was, like Prince Monolulu, a crowd favourite at Epsom, handing out tips to punters for decades, as she did with one racegoer in 1924.

RIGHT: At the height of her Hollywood fame, superstar actress Elizabeth Taylor paid a visit to Sandown Park for a Variety Club meeting, to the evident delight of an enthusiastic crowd.

Footballers have long been associated with racing. Several, such as Sir Alex Ferguson and Michael Owen, have turned their love of the turf into a professional interest by becoming owners, while Mick Channon, Francis Lee and Mick Quinn became trainers. In December 1969, Manchester United's Willie Morgan placed a bet at Haydock.

No Royal Ascot meeting seemed to be complete between the 1960s and the 1990s without an outlandish appearance from Mrs Gertrude Shilling. Sporting spectacular hats designed by her milliner son David, Mrs Shilling became a racecourse institution – she was even nicknamed the "Ascot Mascot".

Her first hat was a comparatively modest 3ft-wide concoction, but later models included hats styled as a piano, giraffe, a dartboard and even a snooker cue and set of balls. In 1970 she wore an elaborately feathered hat for Ladies Day, while she was in patriotic, Union Jack-flying mood in 1982, following the Falklands War.

Ascot Ladies

BELOW: Mrs Shilling wows the Ascot Ladies Day competition in 1970.

ABOVE: Sue Snowdon in 1970.

LEFT: Heidi Douglas, wife of Aston Villa FC chairman "Deadly" Doug – or as the caption writers at the time had it "Mrs Douglas Ellis".

On the traditional start to the flat racing season at Doncaster in 1977, Hortense – the world's fastest tortoise – was pitted against a competitive field thanks to a creative *Daily Mirror* photographer.

The Real Galloping Gourmet

Clement Freud was a man of many and wide-ranging talents. The grandson of philosopher Sigmund Freud, he was an MP, author, an accomplished gourmet and also an ardent racing fan. As well as writing a column for the *Racing Post*, he owned racehorses for a number of years and was a member of the Royal Ascot Racing Club.

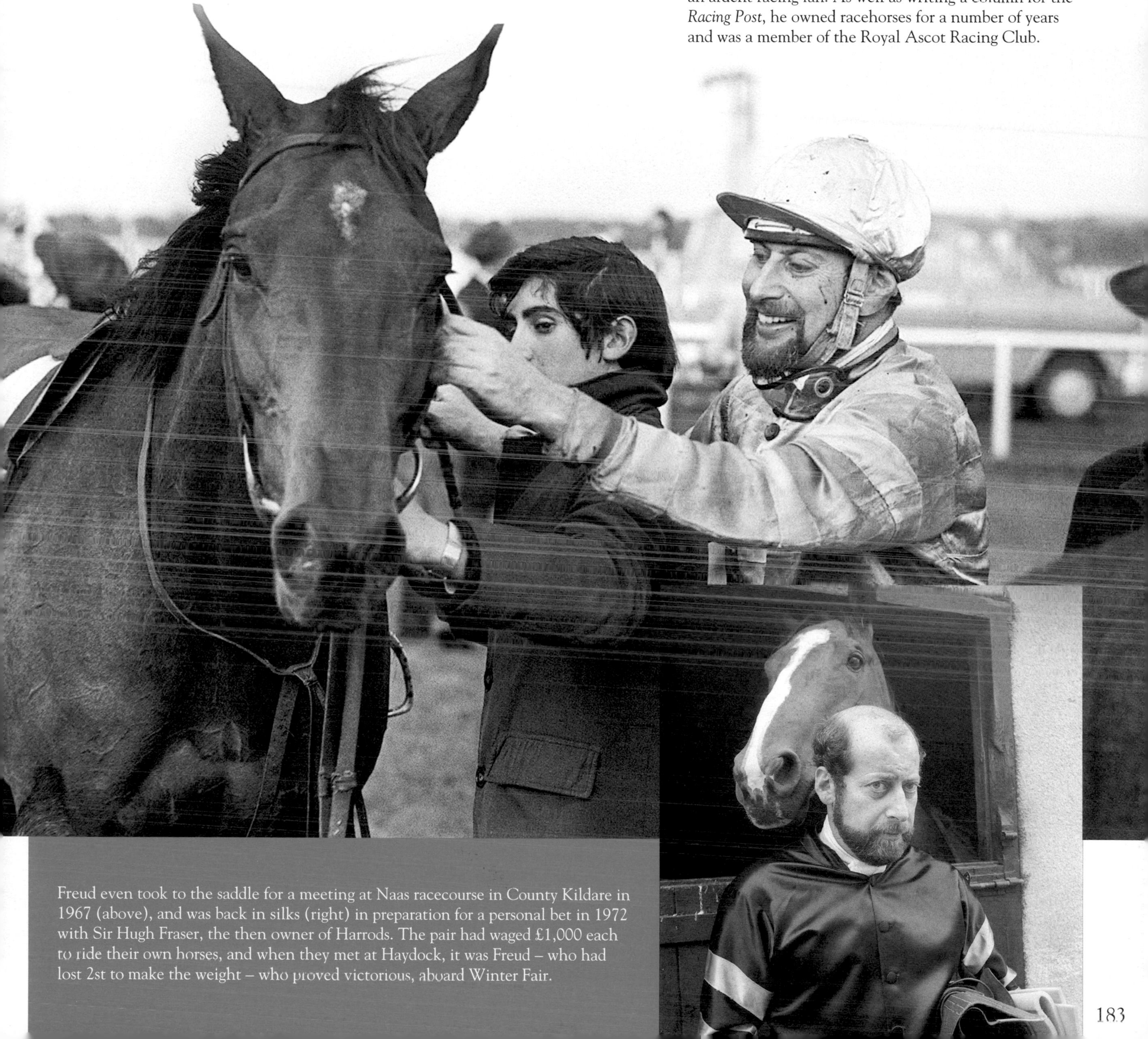

Freud even took to the saddle for a meeting at Naas racecourse in County Kildare in 1967 (above), and was back in silks (right) in preparation for a personal bet in 1972 with Sir Hugh Fraser, the then owner of Harrods. The pair had waged £1,000 each to ride their own horses, and when they met at Haydock, it was Freud – who had lost 2st to make the weight – who proved victorious, aboard Winter Fair.

Racing has enjoyed a long and often illustrious journalistic history …

ABOVE: The *Daily Mirror*'s horse-racing pundit Bob Butchers fixed the cameraman with an intense look at Kempton Park in 1972.

RIGHT: The inimitable, indefatigable John McCririck.

Peter O'Sullevan was arguably racing's greatest commentator. His expert knowledge, articulate delivery and distinctive tones made him, for many punters, the voice of racing: for half a century at the BBC, it was O'Sullevan who brilliantly described many of the sport's most memorable, dramatic and climactic moments.

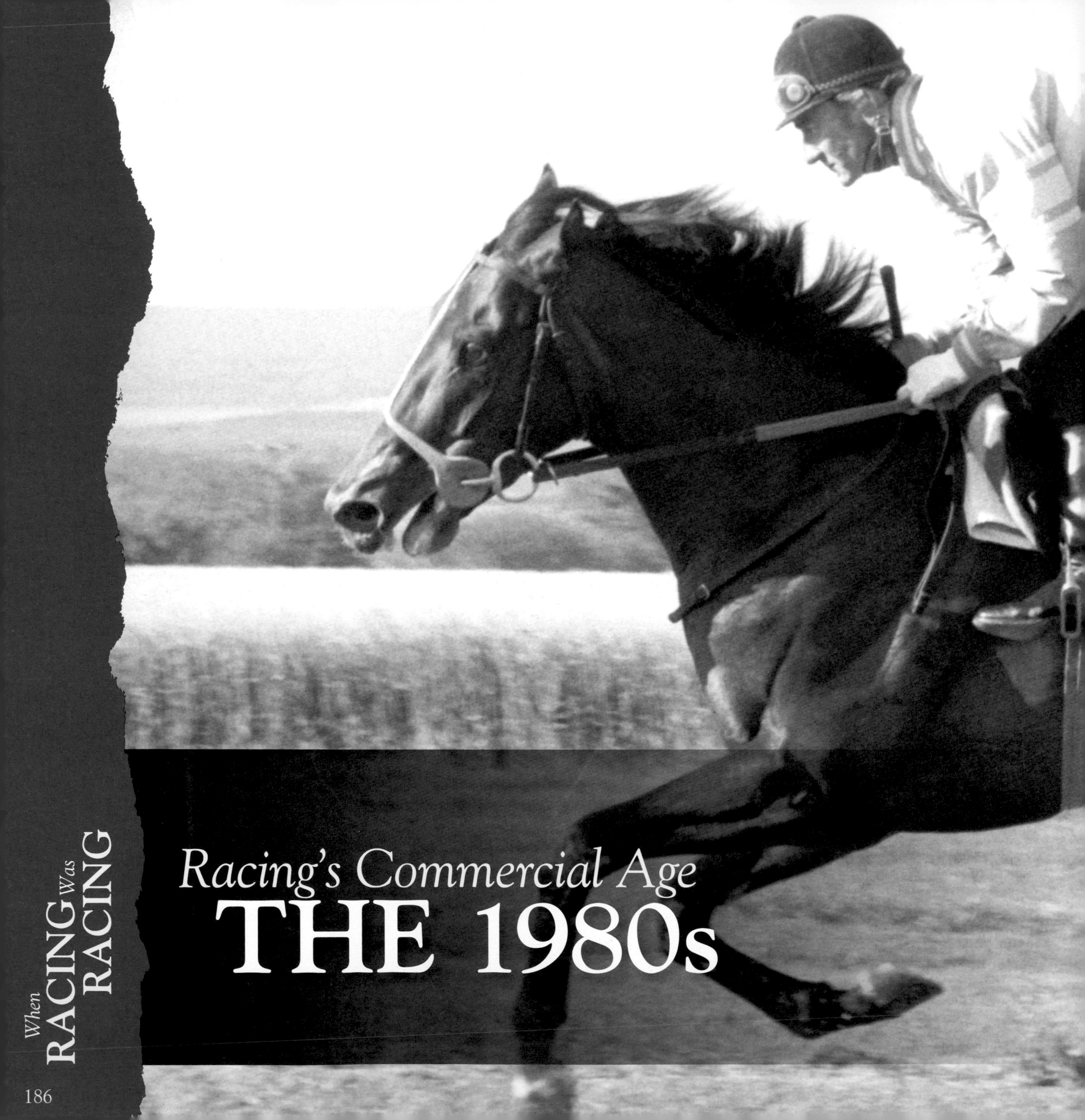

Racing's Commercial Age THE 1980s

Dancing Brave in training in 1986. This was the year when the colt was European Horse of the Year, with victories in the 2000 Guineas, the Eclipse, the King George VI and Queen Elizabeth Stakes, and the Prix de l'Arc de Triomphe. Owned by the Saudi royal Prince Khalid Abdullah, Dancing Brave was put out to stud but, in a sign of changing times, was then sold to Japanese owners in 1991.

In a decade when commercialization and the pursuit of profit became more marked in the wider world, racing reflected the society it operated in, taking on a harder, more business-oriented edge. Vast sums were exchanged for top flat horses – reflecting the profits to be made from their stud value – billionaire owners spent lavishly on huge racing operations, and sponsors snapped up opportunities to promote their products and services via the medium of racing. But amid the money, the sport still produced some memorable moments.

Willie Carson dominated the flat in **1980**, winning the Derby, the 2000 Guineas and the Oaks on the way to becoming Champion Jockey. The same year Sea Pigeon finally gained revenge on his old rival Monksfield – who'd beaten him into second in the previous two runnings – when rounding off the so-called "Golden Age of hurdling" by winning the Champion Hurdle under Jonjo O'Neill. Sea Pigeon followed up by winning again at the age of 11, this time under a sublime and famous ride from John Francome, in **1981**. Other famous names also made their mark that year: Aldaniti and Bob Champion completed an emotional victory at the Grand National, while Shergar and 19-year-old Walter Swinburn won the Derby by a record margin.

Forty-eight-year-old Dick Saunders was a popular winner of the **1982** National aboard Grittar, but in **1983** Shergar was kidnapped from owner Aga Khan's Irish stud, supposedly for ransom purposes. To further emphasize the rocketing value of bloodstock, while El Gran Senor was pipped at the post in the **1984** Derby by Secreto, victory in the Irish Derby propelled the sale price of the son of Northern Dancer to $40 million.

Steve Cauthen repeated his successes in his native America with a superb front-running win on Slip Anchor in the **1985** Derby, while the much-loved Dawn Run completed an unprecedented double when she won the **1986** Cheltenham Gold Cup to add to the Champion Hurdle she had won two years before. She was to die after a fall at Auteuil later in the year.

Henry Cecil confirmed his pre-eminence as a trainer with a remarkable total of seven winners at Royal Ascot to set a new record in **1987**. Martin Pipe forged a similar winning trail in National Hunt, as his long-term jockey partner Peter Scudamore recorded the fastest century of victories in a season, with a win at Haydock Park in December **1988**.

The decade closed in **1989** with the first race on an all-weather track in Britain (at Lingfield) and two landmark triumphs. Nashwan gave trainer Dick Hern his third Derby victory, while Desert Orchid, arguably the most charismatic horse of this or any age, won a famous Cheltenham Gold Cup.

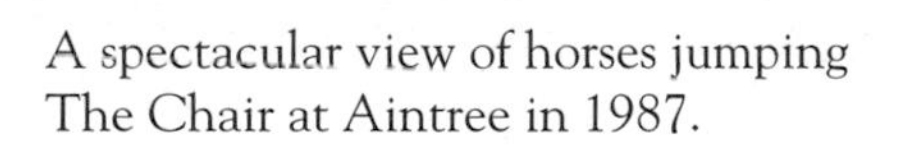

A spectacular view of horses jumping The Chair at Aintree in 1987.

Shergar at rest, three days after his Derby win in 1981. This magnificent animal was to meet a tragic end in one of the most infamous fates ever to befall a racehorse. After his superb Epsom triumph (right), when he trounced the rest of the field and won by a record 10 lengths, and then a disappointing fourth in the St Leger, he was retired to the Ballymany Stud in County Kildare.

In February 1983, the world was stunned when Shergar was kidnapped by masked armed men. A ransom of £2 million was demanded, which soon fell to just £40,000, but the money was never paid and the horse never recovered. While the outcome has never been fully proved, it is likely that Shergar was taken by members of the IRA to a remote countryside spot, and, once it was realized that a ransom would not be received, was killed and buried in an unmarked location – a bloody and cruel end for a hugely popular horse.

SIR FRANCIS DRAKE
DAILY Mirror
HOSPITAI GOES ON A SPREE
SHERGAR £2m ransom riddle
Demos greet Bush
BL freeze ends
Race storm looms again
briefing
Water chiefs turn down new peace bid
MirrorComment
Fleecing the Few
WEATHER
Comfort
Valentine's Day
What will really set her heart aquiver?
Answer
MP talks on for 11 hours
So easy as four gunmen
FIRST-BORN SON: Shergar's week-old foal, so like his famous father.
SHERGAR
OWNER: Aga Khan
Don't harm my champ!
Marched

–LEGENDS–

Willie Carson

An infectious personality as well as a top jockey, Willie Carson completed the transition from fame in his own field to become a highly popular figure in British public life. His distinctive high-pitched laugh and ready wit has made him a natural for television – never more so than when he took part in the series *I'm A Celebrity – Get Me Out of Here!* in 2011 – but his amenable nature belies the toughness of a true competitor.

Born in Stirling, Carson was apprenticed to Gerald Armstrong and won his first race in 1962. From then on, he maintained a consistent and highly successful career for nearly 35 years. At 5ft tall and comfortably able to maintain his riding weight of 7st 10lb – very light for such a power-packed jockey – Carson was also a skilful rider. He was adept at judging pace, timing and tactics, and his many talents found their just reward. He won every English Classic and was a multiple winner at home and abroad, most notably in tandem with trainer Major Dick Hern.

The two forged a terrific partnership, exemplified by Derby wins on Troy (1979), Henbit (1980) and Nashwan (1989), and a famous double of the Oaks and St Leger in the Queen's colours on the filly Dunfermline during the Jubilee year of 1977. When an ailing Hern was unceremoniously removed from her stables in 1989, Carson won wide admiration for his comments in support of his long-standing partner.

When Carson took over the Minster Stud in Cirencester he gained the distinction of being the first jockey in the 20th century to both breed and ride a Classic-winning horse – as Minster Son won the 1988 St Leger. Carson also drew on his wealth of experience, knowledge and insight to bring informed expertise to his work as a racing pundit.

RACING –STATS–

Willie Carson

Name: Willie Carson

Born: 1942

Wins: 3,828

Highlights: Four Derby winners; winner of 17 Classics; Champion Jockey five times

> *Racing has been very good to me.*
>
> – Willie Carson

LEFT: The diminutive Carson took steps to be interviewed by the BBC's 6ft 2in Christopher Powell after victory in France in 1980.

BELOW: Carson enjoyed a healthy rivalry with Lester Piggott. "[He] was a great man to ride against and it was always satisfying to beat him," said Carson. The two went toe-to-toe for the 1980 Jockey Championship, and were pictured together in contrasting moods at Sandown in October. It was the Scotsman who was to head the list by the season's end.

One of the most popular of all race wins came in 1981 with Bob Champion's Grand National victory on Aldaniti. Both horse and rider had been written off – Champion had recovered from cancer after being given just months to live, Aldaniti had battled back from debilitating injuries that might have seen other horses destroyed.

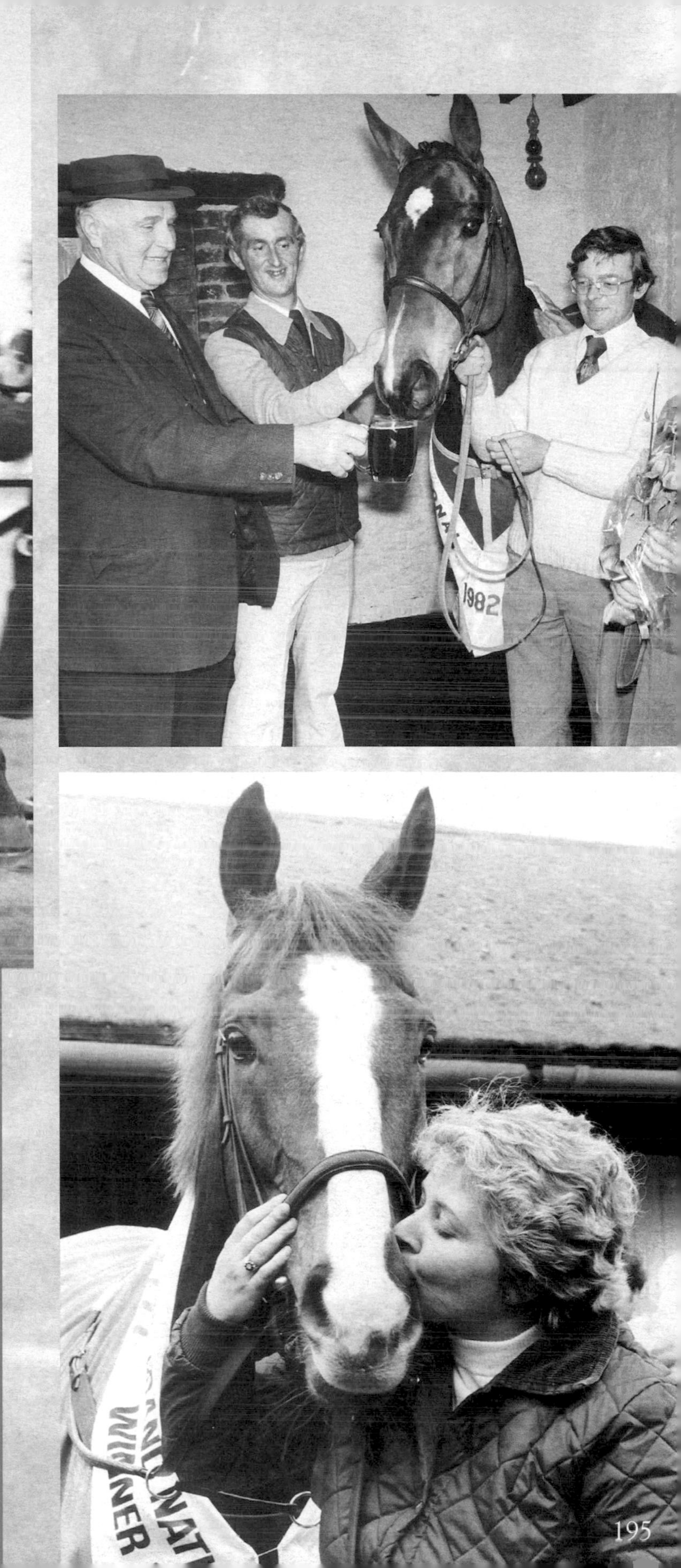

ABOVE: Grittar's victory under Dick Saunders was another Grand National that captured the imagination. At 48, Saunders was the oldest jockey to win the race, and the success was duly celebrated (above right). The day was also notable for Geraldine Rees becoming the first female rider to complete the National.

RIGHT: In 1983, Corbiere got a kiss from Jenny Pitman, the first woman to train a winner of the National. Pitman's then husband Richard had narrowly missed out on his own National as a jockey, when he rode Crisp to a heartbreaking second to Red Rum in 1973.

Sea Pigeon, one of the most popular dual-purpose horses of all time, faced the camera at his Malton stables.

ABOVE: Weighing in in March 1985 was Jonjo O'Neill. The Irishman has been one of the most successful competitors in modern racing. As a jump jockey, he rode 901 winners, including outstanding pairings with Dawn Run and Sea Pigeon. Turning to training (above right), he became the only man to record 100 victories both as a trainer and jockey.

RIGHT: Stable lad Andy Easton gave a cup of tea to West Tip, winner of the 1986 Grand National.

Steve Cauthen (left, with then girlfriend Amy – they later married) was one of the new breed of jockeys to dominate on the flat.

A success in America, he arrived in England at the age of just 18, and hit the ground running. Riding for owner Robert Sangster and trainer Barry Hills, Cauthen won his first UK race with his first mount in 1979 and proceeded to sweep the board. After switching to Henry Cecil's stable, Cauthen's first Derby win came on Slip Anchor in 1985 (right). In a brilliant victory, the horse led from start to finish and simply trounced the opposition.

By the time Cauthen retired, he had won Derby races in four countries – Britain, the USA, France and Ireland.

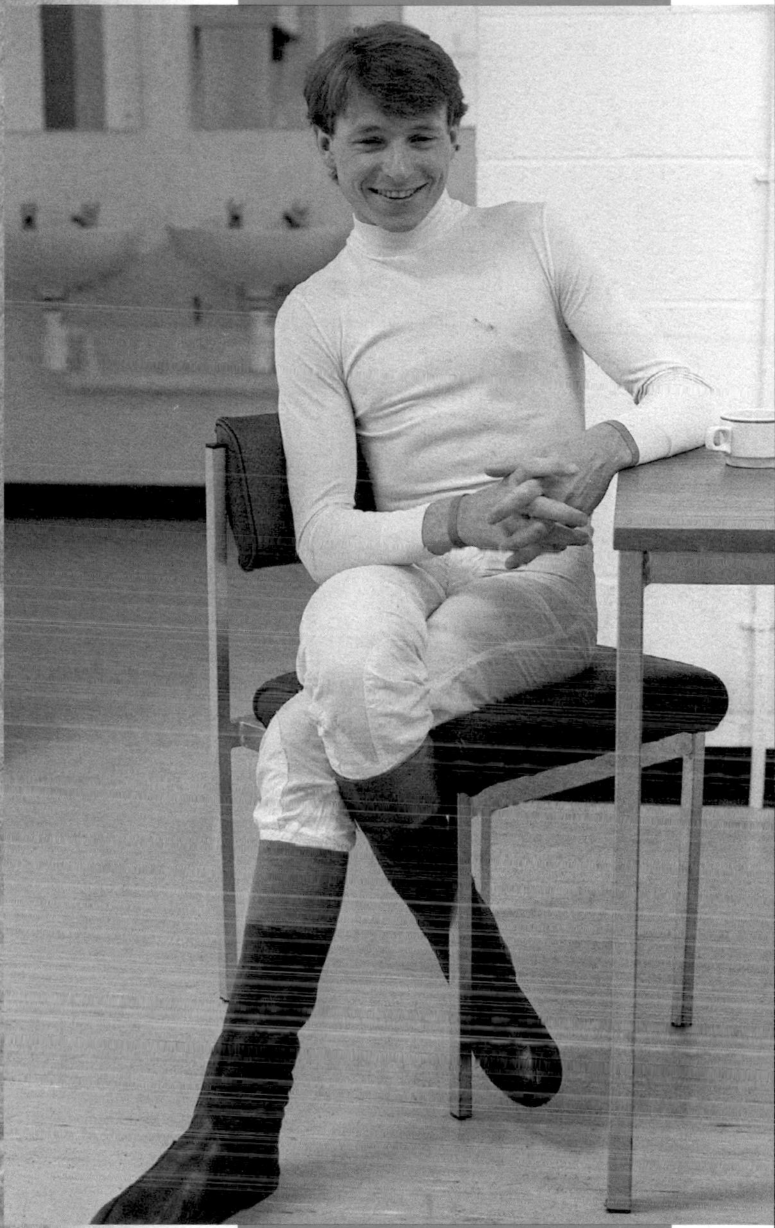

ABOVE: Taking it easy before a race at Kempton in July 1987.

ABOVE: "Here are the fastest pair of colts ever to race over the hallowed turf of Cheltenham" ran the original caption – in this case referring to two Colt helicopters that in 1981 had been brought in to try and help dry out the sodden ground with the downdraft from their rotors.

RIGHT: Give us a kiss: Black Minstrel puckered up for a smacker from stable lad Howard Thomas at the Lambourn yard in 1980.

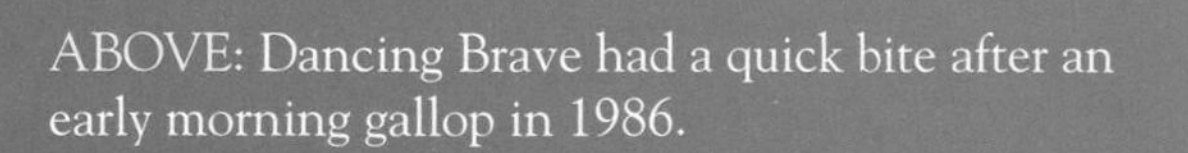

ABOVE: Dancing Brave had a quick bite after an early morning gallop in 1986.

RIGHT: Lester Piggott's ninth Derby victory came in 1983, when he led Teenoso home. Four years later, the great man was jailed for tax evasion.

FAR RIGHT: Nashwan's Derby win in 1989 was one of the 1980s' most impressive and popular victories, with both jockey Willie Carson and trainer Dick Hern crowd favourites. It was also the first Derby success for owner Sheikh Hamdan bin Rashid Al Maktoum.

–LEGENDS–

Desert Orchid

Desert Orchid in full, glorious flight was one of the most unforgettable sporting sights of the late 1980s. Not only did ardent racegoers cherish his displays, but even those with only the most cursory interest in the track were thrilled by his exploits. His strength, determination and bravery were self-evident; the way he attacked fences and cleared them with a stylish flourish made for a breathtaking sight; and, of course, his handsome grey livery simply made him look spectacular.

Though "Dessie" fell on his racecourse debut over hurdles, he subsequently did very well in that discipline, but it was when he tackled the bigger jumps afforded by a switch to chasing that he really came into his own. He produced a resounding 15-length victory in the King George in 1986 (he won it a record four times in all) and thereafter dominated the National Hunt headlines. Trained by David Elsworth and ridden first by Colin Brown and then by Simon Sherwood and Richard Dunwoody, Desert Orchid recorded a succession of famous wins, until he faced the ultimate test with the Gold Cup in 1989.

Cheltenham did not suit him. Dessie preferred right-handers to the left-handed Cheltenham course, while snow and rain had made the going utterly unsuited to his flamboyant style. And yet, displaying reserves of courage and physical strength, a mud-spattered Dessie overcame Yahoo in the final slog up the hill to win by a length and a half. The huge crowd of 58,000 went mad – rarely can there have been a more popular and charismatic winner of any race.

Like Red Rum before him, Desert Orchid retired from racing to enjoy a spell as a celebrity. He was held in enormous affection until his peaceful death in 2006.

His grey coat spattered with mud, Dessie takes a well-earned breather after the epic 1989 Cheltenham Gold Cup.

RACING
-STATS-
Desert Orchid

Name: Desert Orchid
Born: 1979
Died: 2006
Races: 70
Wins: 34
Highlights: Cheltenham Gold Cup 1989; King George VI Chase 1986, 1988–90

> *Desert Orchid and I have a lot in common. We are both greys, vast sums of money are riding on our performance, the Opposition hopes we shall fall at the first fence and we are both carrying too much weight.*
>
> – Norman Lamont, then Chancellor of the Exchequer, 1991

ABOVE: Dessie checking his fan mail.

BELOW: Visiting inmates at Ashwell Prison in 1990.

7
5

LEFT: In one of the most iconic races of the 1980s – indeed, of all racing history – Desert Orchid, ridden by Simon Sherwood, is pictured on his mud-spattered way to first place in the 1989 Cheltenham Gold Cup. It was a heroic performance that also represented a magnificent achievement for trainer David Elsworth and owner Richard Burridge.

Acknowledgements

Special thanks to Mel Cullinan for his expert knowledge, sound advice, inspired suggestions and invaluable patience.

Further special thanks to Vito Inglese, Dave Scripps and all at Mirrorpix for their superb assistance with picture research, and, as always, to Richard Havers for his support and expert advice.

Thank you also to Paul Moreton, Kevin Gardner and all at Haynes, and Elizabeth Stone and Becky Ellis.

Select bibliography

The author is indebted to many and varied sources for facts, figures and confirmations. The limitations of space constrain the number cited, but the following have proved invaluable:

Bill Mooney and George Ennor, *The Complete Encyclopedia of Horse Racing* (5th edn, Carlton Books, 2011).

Norman Barrett (ed.), *The Daily Telegraph Chronicle of Horse Racing* (Guinness, 1995).

Elwyn Hartley Edwards, *Racehorse: The Complete Guide to Horse Racing* (AA, 2008).

Sean Magee, *Arkle: The Life and Legacy of "Himself"* (Highdown, 2005).

Daily Mirror

Guardian/Observer

Independent

The BBC

Daily Telegraph

Racing Post